Pieter Bruegel the Elder and Lucas van Leyden

The Complete Engravings, Etchings, and Woodcuts

Jacques Lavalleye

Pieter Bruegel the Elder and Lucas van Leyden

The Complete Engravings, Etchings, and Woodcuts

Harry N. Abrams, Inc., Publishers, New York

Jacket design by Wim Crouwel

Library of Congress Catalog Card Number: 67–18090

All rights reserved. No part of the contents of this book may be reproduced
without the written permission of the publishers,
Harry N. Abrams, Incorporated, New York.
Plates printed in France · Text printed in Holland · Bound in Holland

Lucas van Leyden

Three strong artistic personalities dominate engraving in the first thirty years of the sixteenth century: Albrecht Dürer, Marcantonio Raimondi, and Lucas van Leyden. Of the three, Lucas van Leyden had the shortest life, dying in the early 1530's, and yet his contemporaries recognized him as a master, tireless and endowed with a rich creative imagination, an engraver of rare originality and incomparable technique. Tradition confirms this admiration for his prints, which were often rare and over which collectors fought to pay high prices. Through the centuries the work of Van Leyden has been consistently regarded as an authentic expression of precociousness and of inspiration.

Like other equally individual artists, Lucas van Leyden had no real descendants. He was copied—engravers, painters, and workers in stained glass were inspired by his compositions—but he had no disciples. The glory of having been the first Dutch artist to enjoy a worldwide reputation suffices. It is curious to note that like Rembrandt, who was also a native of Leyden, Lucas is generally known by his first name, and this link is strengthened in that they both combine typically national traits with universal characteristics.

Contemporary archives preserved at Leyden and the *Book of the Painters*, published by Karel van Mander in 1604, are the chief sources that enable one to trace the stages in the life of Lucas Hugensz.

He was born in Leyden in modest circumstances. His father, Hugh Jacobsz. van Leyden, no doubt a Mannerist painter, had married the daughter of the local organist, Dirk Florisz. Van Mander gives the year of Lucas' birth as 1494, but Pelinck has advanced valid arguments for putting this date back to 1489 (*Oud Holland*, 1949, p. 193).

Nothing is known for certain of his formative years. Revealing slightly naïve enthusiasm lacking in critical judgment, Van Mander wrote on this topic that "Lucas, a master from the cradle, was trained first by his father and later by Cornelis Engelbrechtsz. Driven equally by his inclination and his love of art, he showed extraordinary application, working by night as well as by day. For toys he had the instruments of his profession: charcoal, crayons, pens, paint brushes, the engraver's needle. For friends he chose young painters, glassworkers, or goldsmiths. How often did his mother try to stop him from drawing through the night, not because she was so concerned at the cost of the candles, but at the effect of sleepless nights and the mental strain on the frail constitution of the young man." The imaginative chronicler goes on that "at the age of twelve he painted on canvas, in distemper, *The Legend of St. Hubert*, a prodigious work that instantly gave him a great name. Lord Lockhorst acquired this picture and for it paid him as many gold sovereigns as he had years." It is also maintained that the young artist received his initial training in engraving by frequenting the workshop first of a craftsman specializing in the inlaying of weapons and later that of a goldsmith. The names of these craftsmen are not given.

Whatever his early background, 1508 marks Lucas' first dated print, entitled *The Drunkenness of Mohammed*, while his oldest recorded picture, *The Temptation of St. Anthony*, at the Royal Museum of Art in Brussels, bears the date 1511. These two works, produced by the young artist at fourteen and seventeen years of age, respectively, or according to a more likely recent chronology nineteen and twenty-two, are recognized as masterpieces. Now these masterpieces must clearly have been preceded by and have developed from Lucas' first and no doubt rapidly developing attempts at engraving and printing.

Around 1517 he married Lysbeth van Boschhuysen, a young girl from an eminent family of Leyden. The marriage produced no children, but there is record of the existence of an illegitimate daughter, Marijten, who married the painter Dammes Claesz. from Utrecht.

While the town of Leyden, depressed since the end of the fifteenth century through the decline of the wool industry, was emerging from the nightmare years of 1509–20, during which floods and an outbreak of the plague had taken heavy toll of its inhabitants, Lucas left for Antwerp. One cannot be sure of the precise date of Lucas' stay or stays in the rapidly expanding Brabantine city, where he established good relations with the artists and the publishers for whom he worked.

It was in Antwerp that he met Albrecht Dürer in June, 1521. An entry in the Nuremburg master's diary of his journey noted that Master Lucas, copper engraver, had issued him an invitation. He gives a profile of Lucas: "He is a quite small man, a native of Leyden." On the twelfth he adds, "I have sketched Master Lucas." This refers to his portrait in silver on treated white paper, a magnificent drawing from the Wicar collection at the Museum of Fine Arts in Lille. In it Lucas appears relatively thin, hollow-cheeked, with wide-open eyes and an animated, penetrating look. He is wearing expensive, elegant clothes. Finally Dürer notes the exchange of engravings made by himself and Lucas. "I have exchanged all Lucas' engravings for eight florins' worth of my art." In 1522, no doubt as a mere formality, "meester Lucas de Hollandere schildere" was registered with the St. Luke Guild of painters in Antwerp.

If one accepts Pelinck's chronology, it was in 1522 and not in 1527 that Lucas undertook with the painter Jean Gossart a journey through Zeeland, Flanders, and Brabant, visiting Middelburg, Ghent, and Malines on his return to Antwerp. Van Mander describes this episode, emphasizing that the thirty-three-year-old Lucas liked to dress with studied elegance, wearing a costume of fine yellow camelot that shone in the sun like gold; he used to invite the painters of the town he was visiting to costly banquets and received them with great ceremony.

Van Mander also reports that this journey exhausted him and weakened his health, which was beginning to fail. This did not prevent him from accepting in 1526 a flattering commission for *The Last Judgment*, which decorated the Baptismal Chapel of the Church of St. Peter in Leyden (at present in the Stedelijk Museum "De Lakenhal"). His ill health did not affect the output of his engraving until the last months of his life.

Always feverish, often bedridden—Van Mander wonders if he was suffering from tuberculosis— and weakened not just by illness but by overwork, Lucas burnt himself out. It seems that he was unable to complete his print *Pallas Athene*. He died in Leyden in 1533, aged thirty-nine if it is true that he was born in 1494, or aged forty-four if one accepts his birth date as 1489.

Cornelis Engelbrechtsz., born in 1468, who is said to have been Lucas' tutor until 1508 and was the strongest personality among the Mannerist painters in Leyden, also died in 1533. Jacob Cornelisz. van Oostsanen, who was born about 1470, was another who died in 1533. Several woodcuts that some critics class as Lucas' work are also attributed to this master of the Mannerist School at Amsterdam. Van Oostsanen, who belonged to a younger generation, though he too died in 1533, succeeded in making use of, without adopting, the enervated, insipid criteria of a belated Gothicism. His strong and original personality enabled him to work out for himself the problems that faced the period, and it was as an individual that he tackled the choices offered by the Renaissance.

Before undertaking an analysis of Lucas' engravings and noting their various characteristics, it is wise to make a more systematic study of his artistic relationships.

An examination of his first prints reveals surprisingly little connection between his work and the engravings of his Dutch predecessors and contemporaries. At the very most one can maintain that the set of nine woodcuts, "The Round Passion," seems to show a little of the influence of Cornelis Engelbrechtsz.

Lucas' major encounter on an artistic level was that with the work of Albrecht Dürer and later with the artist himself, though the meeting did not take place until 1521. The engravings of the Nuremburg master had spread to Leyden well before his journey of 1520–21 and had assured him an indisputable reputation. The young artists in the studios of the painters and engravers and the offices of the editors certainly had time to examine, discuss, and admire the Frankish engraver's abundant artistic creations. It can reasonably be supposed, for example, that Nicolas Hogenberg, Jacopo de' Barbari, and many others had brought back to the Low Countries collections of the engravings of Dürer, who was always interested in selling his work everywhere.

There is no doubt that Lucas became acquainted with Dürer's work very early, as is evidenced by a number of his prints executed around 1508, for example, *David Playing the Harp before Saul* and *The Holy Family with Apples*, in which he adopts the planchette, which had been used by Dürer since 1500, to inscribe his monogram. His meeting with Dürer, the understanding that drew them together, the exchange they made of their work, only confirmed Lucas' admiration for his elder, and this contact with the man and his work was beneficial to Lucas. Without going into detail it can be said that Lucas admired the unerring, precise drawing and was inspired by it. From Dürer he also learned to appreciate the beauty of the use of white spaces. He borrowed from him various elements of his compositions, such as the horseman and his horse in *The Triumph of Mordecai* (1515), which is portrayed in reverse to the similar group in the engraving *The Horseman, Death, and the Devil* (1513). *The Standard-Bearer* (1510) is modeled after Dürer's, which dates from before 1500. The fourteen plates, "The Passion of Christ, or the Small Passion" (1521) owe much to the woodcuts of Dürer's "Small Passion" (1507–13), and similarly the *Portrait of the Emperor Maximilian I* is inspired from the woodcut of 1519. It was at the time of

Dürer's journey through the Low Countries that Lucas experimented with the acid technique that the Nuremburg master had already used for years. He executed seven etchings, sometimes touched up with the needle, one in 1518 and six in 1520.

Lucas, always sensitive to innovations, was also influenced by his stay in Antwerp. One knows that the work of most of its painters was strongly marked by Mannerism. Yet, as a painter molded in the workshops of Leyden that also showed this influence would have been most receptive to criteria not altogether unfamiliar to him, it would be unwise to take the traces of Mannerism in Lucas' work as evidence enabling one to date precisely his stay or stays in Antwerp.

In 1913 Beets envisaged the probable year of Lucas' first contact with the wealthy Brabantine city as 1511. This assertion is no longer valid inasmuch that, though none of his engravings bears the actual date, Lucas produced at least one important picture during this year. Thus the artist was active in 1511—a fact unknown to Beets—and did not pass his time traveling without thought of work. Is it the result of a stay in Antwerp, of the influence of Leyden, or even of contact with the engravings of Dürer, that in the set "The Story of Joseph" one notes a new concern with form, a desire for more refined composition, an attempt at more complicated female dress portraying flowing folds, the adoption of the caricatured figure? Added to these characteristics in *Esther before Ahasuerus* (1518) is a touch of affectation, a relaxation of pose, a lengthening of the limbs and bodies, a concern with prettiness, and a cultivation of rich and elaborate finery. The same applies to *The Dance of Magdalen* (1519). The obese, caricatured figure of *The Fool Kissing a Woman* (1520) and the theme itself are doubtless inspired by the characters and themes of Leonardo da Vinci, although they were already used at this time in Antwerp by Quentin Massys and popularized by Jan Massys, among others.

Finally one must consider Lucas' attitude toward the Italian Renaissance. Although like Rembrandt he never visited the peninsula, he was acquainted with the new ideas of a movement at its triumphant zenith in the beginning of the sixteenth century. Through Dürer's engravings and the pictures and drawings of his friend Gossart, Lucas was able to face the problems of the day. But it was the prints of Marcantonio Raimondi that introduced him to the solutions and the models created by the masters of the Italian Renaissance. In several works, especially toward the end of his life, Lucas made good use of the examples brought within his reach. It is in this way that he became more inclined to evoke the plump, rounded shapes of the naked figure, revealing a better knowledge of anatomy and more respect for the laws of proportion. So appear Adam and Eve in "The Story of the First Couple" (1529), the scene of *Original Sin* (1530), and the nude allegories of "The Theological and Cardinal Virtues" (1530). The artist concentrates on more complicated composition and movement, posed positions, charming expressions, notably in *Venus and Cupid* (1529), *Lot and His Daughters* (1530), and *Mars, Venus, and Cupid* (1530). A new interest in mythological themes is evident in his work. The *Cupids* (1517) are no longer considered as decorative elements in a frame, but as naked gods living on Olympus.

Through contact with Raimondi's work Lucas adopted a more impersonal style of drawing that was detrimental to his refined evocation of silvery light and delicate atmosphere, at least in some prints in the evening of his career.

Lucas' engravings are numerous. There are extant today 177 copper engravings bearing his monogram "L," which is upside down eight times; 97 are dated — sometimes the date appears only on the second state. None of these was produced in 1511, 1521, 1526, or after 1530. One can note that between 1512 and 1519 as between 1523 and 1526 his annual output was fairly regular; the years 1520–21, when it is certain that Lucas was in Antwerp, are the most productive, and the same applies to 1530.

The quality of his engravings on copper is superlative. They are often delicate plates possibly limited in number to preserve the silver subtleties and the fineness of line. From this stems the rarity of some of Lucas' prints, notably *The Holy Family* (1508) and *Christ the Saviour* (1510). Sandrart reports that a Swedish collector paid five hundred florins around 1640 to obtain a print from the plate *Abraham Renouncing Hagar* (1508). Similarly Rembrandt bought *The Bohemians* (*Huilenspiegel*, 1520) for the sum of two hundred florins. It is of course true that this inspired artist of the seventeenth century did not stint when he could acquire prints by his famous predecessor.

Examples of his more craftsmanlike woodcuts are less numerous, totaling 110, of which 47 are independent works and 63 book illustrations. The independent woodcuts date from two periods preceding Lucas' journey to Antwerp, 1513–14 and 1517–20. Only three bear the artist's monogram, and as none of these works is dated, the compilation of the list and the chronology can only be established by recourse to comparison, by taking into account the quite important difference in the technique used in engraving by incision and the engraving in relief often adopted by a craftsman limiting himself to making a copy of his master's work. Several works are now extant only in one copy, such as *The Young Woman at the Spinning Wheel* (1513), *The Prodigal Son Carousing* (1519), *Aristotle and Phyllis, St. Peter* (1519), *The Virgin with a Rosary*, and *Christ's Farewell to His Mother* (1518–19).

Lucas van Leyden, like Holbein and many others, was commissioned to illustrate books. Publishers sought him as a contributor. There exist at least 63 of these woodcuts, which were often used in several publications and even passed from one firm to another. They are attributed to Lucas on the basis of stylistic comparison and tradition. It is quite simple to date them by the year of issue of the works in which they are included. From 1508 to 1517 Lucas did a great deal of work for the publisher Jan Seversz. His first illustration, no doubt engraved by Joost de Negker, serves as the frontispiece to the *Breviarum insignis ecclesie Traiectensis*, which came off the press on March 31, 1508. *The Standard of Jan Seversz. at Haarlem* appears in the *Libellus a magistro Petro de Rivo editus. Quomodo omnia in meliore(m) sunt p(ar)te(m) interpretanda* of 1509. The mystical work of the seraphic doctor *Bonaventura. Dit Boeck is gheheten inden latijne Stimulus divini amoris* (1511) includes three pictures. But it was between 1511 and 1514 that Seversz.

commissioned the greatest contribution from Lucas for the *Missale ad veru(m) cathedralis ecclesie Traiectensis ritu(m)*; for this the artist composed 42 religious images, some of which were used again in the *Ortulus anime devotaru(m) orationu(m) flosculis variis refertus* (1515). The last work for which Lucas produced historical illustrations of note was the famous chronicle *Die cronyck van Hollandt, Zeelandt en(de) Vrieslandt* (1517).

Jan Seversz. left Leyden for Antwerp. The editor Willem Vosterman borrowed several woodcuts from him which he reproduced in the Bible that he published in 1528 and in successive editions. And again it was in Antwerp that Henri Peetersen van Middelburch reprinted the Missal of Utrecht Cathedral, still using woodcuts made from Lucas' drawings. This repeated use of the woodcuts did undeniable damage to the originals. The illustrations after 1528 clearly reveal wear and sometimes even traces of wormholes. In addition these woodcuts were used on individual sheets as images of devotion, for example, *Christ on the Cross, between the Virgin and St. John* and *St. Martin Sharing His Coat. St. Dorothy* and *St. Margaret*, on the other hand, must be considered as having been used as illustrations for a book of devotions.

It is difficult to classify Lucas' earliest burin engravings. Rosy Kahn suggested a grouping in 1918, but this scholar's excellent work did not win unanimous support. Critics have accepted Friedländer's proposal to group the first prints between 1505 and 1508.

Trial and error are evident in Lucas' early work. The hard, stiff, and labored outlines of *St. Mary Magdalen in the Desert* clearly show the youthfulness of the engraver. It is of interest to note the corrections that appear in the second state of several of the plates. That of *Abigail before King David* reveals supplementary strokes intended to give a clearer suggestion of light. In *Samson and Delilah* and *The Raising of Lazarus* there are new lines giving more clarity to detail. The outlines are still stiff and clumsy in *Original Sin*, as they are in the woodcut *St. Martin Sharing His Coat*. In other respects, however, one is struck by Lucas' originality of composition, his breadth of outlook, and the life given to his work by its delicate atmosphere. The artist likes to situate his subjects in a vast landscape filled with trees or groups of buildings. He gives the scene depth, keeping the foreground for the principal incident and adding a secondary subject in the background or vice versa. He balances accentuated figures with more delicate, restrained forms in the more distant background, offering his personal solution to one of the problems that was causing concern at the beginning of the sixteenth century, aerial perspective. In *Abigail before King David*, the wife of rich Nabal is approaching the angry king from below in the middle ground. The Philistines, terrified even though they are armed, are waiting cautiously in the background, until the giant's hair is cut in *Samson and Delilah*. At the outskirts of the town, Sarah, her face full of satisfaction, with Isaac beside her, watches *Abraham Renouncing Hagar*, who in full light seems about to leave the scene in her distress, preceded by the young Ishmael carrying his provision bag, while in the background to the right one can make out the angel pointing to the spring that will save them. *St. Christopher on the Bank of a River* is a new interpretation of the theme. Lucas does not portray St. Christopher's actual crossing of the river with the Child on his shoulders, but we see the saint seated, listening to the call coming from the other bank where the Child appears in the distance. Between the two protagonists the hermit is emerging from his cell, carrying a lantern to light his way in the darkness.

Lucas' contemporaries were struck by the importance he gave to nature as a framework. Raimondi was certainly inspired by this aspect of his work. The landscape and the fence to the right in *The Holy Family with Apples* appear in the Italian engraver's *Death of Dido*, and the left section of the background of *St. Mary Magdalen in the Desert* is repeated in his *Pietà*. Already in 1510 Raimondi made use of the landscape and group of trees that appear to the left of *The Drunkenness of Mohammed* (1508) in his famous work *The Climbers*; he takes up the natural setting of *Susannah and the Two Elders* in his *Lucretia*.

Lucas' originality does not lie only in his presentation of subjects but also in his evocation and interpretation of traditional themes. We have just seen that he does not adopt the current representation of St. Christopher. The bull is close to *St. Luke*, but the attribute of the evangelist serves both as a seat and as a desk. The combat with the dragon takes place in the background of *St. George Freeing the Princess*, while highlighted in the foreground is the moving spectacle of the knight dismounting to comfort the young woman before taking his leave. *The Holy Family with Apples*, which already has reflecting high lights, portrays in the foreground an intimate family scene against an admirable, precisely detailed summer landscape. Mary's weariness, Jesus' childish trust, and Joseph's solicitude combine to make it a portrayal rich in human truth.

Lucas was passionately interested in the human figure. In his early works his shapes are heavy and sometimes gross. The difficulty he found in drawing heads that are thrown back, seen foreshortened, or from above is evident in *The Raising of Lazarus, David in Prayer*, and *The Holy Family*. His first nudes lack suppleness and reveal an as yet incomplete knowledge of anatomy and the mechanics of the muscles, as can be seen by an analysis of *Original Sin* and in the figure of the Child Jesus playing naked beside *The Holy Family*. But what excites Lucas are the movements, the behavior, the intentions, and the character of man. We can visualize the young artist observing his contemporaries, following them in the town or in the country, and then sketching from life poses and expressions against a framework of nature or a cluster of buildings so as to portray them accurately and realistically. Lucas adopted this genre setting from the start and did not hesitate to situate religious and biblical subjects against these backgrounds that gave him good opportunity to represent the variations of human psychology and temperament. For example, there are the studied poses of *The Lady* [wearing ancient Burgundian dress] *and the Gentleman with a Falcon*, of the *Four Soldiers in the Forest*, and *The Pilgrims* in the abandon of rest watching with pleasurable anticipation the peeling of a pear that will quench their thirst, while in the background another pilgrim passes reciting his rosary. We come now to *The Farewell Kiss*, a print which Bartsch does not discuss. Does it portray a biblical scene? Is it one of Lot's daughters, accompanied by a lady of standing carrying a casket on her head, bidding farewell to her lover who is not leaving Sodom? Or more simply, is it the moment of separation of a young woman turning back toward her suitor who kisses her respectfully on the lips? Next there is *The Woman and the Man with a Torch Followed by a Fool*, which is certainly a scene of love and humor. The young torchbearer is tightly clasping the waist of the girl who seems absorbed in melancholy thoughts; they are followed by a fool, while a man watches the couple from a window. It is the first time that a scene by torchlight appears in an engraving in Holland.

The Drunkenness of Mohammed bears the date 1508. Lucas executed this work either at the age of fourteen or nineteen. It is a rarely treated subject, inspired by a tale of travel famous in the Middle Ages written by Jean de Mandeville after a journey to the Middle East in 1327. The artist creates a masterpiece from the theme. The prophet is sleeping heavily, while his servant is carefully placing on his left knee his master's sword that he has used to kill the monk Sergius, Mohammed's friend. The holy man is lying crookedly with his throat slashed. Groups of people are in conversation near a river with a mountain scene enlivened by castles and other buildings in the distance. When Mohammed wakes up, unable to remember what he did or did not do in his drunkenness, he will make the decision to forbid his followers to drink wine. An enormous sealed gourd hangs symbolically from the branch of a tree. The figures are well formed, the poses true to life, and the diffusion of light remarkable because of the subtle play of the delicate hachures and the judicious distribution of whites among the blacks and halftones. The atmosphere is transparent right to the tops of the mountains, flowing over the wooden walls and the thatch of the cottage on the right. The virtuoso engraver asserts all his early mastery in this plate, which has silver high lights in his best style. *Susannah and the Two Elders* is in the same vein. The originality of this plate lies as much in the presentation and conception of the theme, in the construction of the scene, as in the evocation of the imponderable atmosphere. The two bourgeois are not yet too old to feel the torment of desire as they watch Susannah bathe her feet in the clear stream. Lucas achieves the same suppleness and fluency in the clothes of the young watcher as in the habit of the monk killed by Mohammed's servant.

In *David Playing the Harp before Saul* Lucas retains only the human figures, which he encloses in a small, restricted space. The figures are seen close-up and for the first time are conceived on a larger scale. He has created living individuals whose poses and expressions are a true guide to their feelings and behavior. Saul is tortured and oppressed, he can hardly bear the menace weighing him down, his eyes express hate, and his mouth is contorted. Yet he seems to be hesitating. Could this not be the effect of the music that the young, stocky David is plucking nervously from his harp? Although calm, his eyes are drawn toward Saul. At the front of an anonymous crowd one notes a man wearing a bonnet listening to the arguments of a young man (could it be Lucas himself explaining the incident?).

Lucas' first period ends in 1509–10, with the artist showing greater fluency of composition and more virtuosity in depicting crowds on a larger scale, as well as a now completely developed skill in portraying true-to-life characters belonging to different social classes.

Christ the Saviour in a niche, of which only one copy survives, is portrayed with his loins girded by a perizonium, which is entangled in the swirling folds of a cloak that serves as a background to this somewhat academic nude, whereas "Christ and the Apostles" are heavily clad. But in this series of devotional illustrations Lucas tries to vary the poses and the personalities of the faces, which in the case of the apostles stand out from enormous decorative halos. The naked body of *St. Sebastian* is much more sensitively portrayed and given delicate tones by the light. He is attached to a tree whose dark trunk follows exactly the pose of the martyr's body, while a second tree rises highlighted in the middle ground. This plate is more an engraver's exercise than a devotional image. The same applies to *The Standard-Bearer*, which is modeled after Dürer's. In the accurate proportions, the outline and rendering of the figures, Lucas gives it a more sensitive treatment and achieves a more delicate balance between light and shade.

The human figure interests Lucas more than ever, as much in its physical as in its psychological aspect. *The Woman with a Hind* (1508) brings to mind Dürer's model; for Lucas she affords a pretext to portray in profile the soft lines of a naked woman. *Seated Woman with a Dog* (1510) is also naked and fat; she is applying herself with great concentration to her task of picking fleas from the dog, a task facilitated by the passiveness of the animal. It is the portrait of a common woman with the body of a fertile goddess in repose. *The Milkmaid* (1510) is a real peasant woman about to milk the cattle that are awaiting the moment of relief. She is advancing barefoot, carrying in her hands the necessary equipment. One cow is portrayed sideways, while a dull-faced cowherd is paying more attention to the young farmgirl, whose eyes are modestly lowered, than to the beast that needs to be kept calm. One does not know what to praise most in this famous plate: the grace of the rustic scene, the magnificent realistic portrayal of the animals, the expert highlighting of figures and cattle, or the elements of the landscape. Or even the originality of treating such a scene. For thirty years later Paul Potter, Albert Cuyp, and Adrien van de Velde were to take up this type of genre scene exalting animals. But did they show such delicacy and deep feeling for pastoral serenity? Could the two common-looking men in *Two Couples in the Wood* be, as Fritz Lugt suggests, "bandit gallants"? Their female companions show a little more distinction. The first, clasped round the waist, is conversing with dignity, while her companion seems rather tired or even disappointed by her less interested gallant. *The Mendicants* could be either beggars or thirsty pilgrims carrying waterskins, beggars' satchels, rosaries, and staves. There is more activity here than in *The Pilgrims*, just as *A Young Man with Eight Armed Men* is more animated and tells more of a story than the *Four Soldiers in the Forest*.

The Temptation of St. Anthony (1509) is rightly considered one of the young Lucas' most remarkable works. A woman is seen in profile from the left, standing out against a delicate receding landscape, and is addressing herself to the saint with apparent calm. She is elegantly dressed. Contrasting with the apparent serenity of her face, her bonnet has horns, the attributes of the devil. This woman, symbolizing the tempter, is offering a vase of perfume to the holy man. A group of sturdy trees whose branches break up the sky cuts the scene in two, and a table made of rocks separates the personages. The hermit, seated in profound thought, interrupts his reading and with a dignified gesture is blessing the apparition. Although he seems calm and in control of himself, his left hand resting on his book and his toes reveal his real nervousness. His chapel, the rocks, the woods, a castle barring the horizon to the left, each represents a different plane through the subtle play of the lines. This variation of dimension, thus of light and shade, also occurs in the more animated *Adam and Eve after the Expulsion from the Garden of Eden* (1510). The landscape is dominated by a cold and gusty wind, Adam is carrying a heavy implement on his shoulder, and with his right hand is pushing on Eve, who is holding, huddled close to her, her first-born Cain.

In 1509 Lucas produced the first of many plates composed on a larger scale and containing more figures, *The Conversion of St. Paul*. In the foreground Saul is continuing his journey to Damascus with an armed escort, no longer in order to persecute the Christians but to have himself baptized there. Blinded by the divine light, he has to be led by his companions who cannot take their eyes off him and are discussing the event they have just witnessed. This varied troop is portrayed in front of a mass of rock forming a screen, to the right of which can be seen a valley leading to an imposing castle. On the other side, the earlier episode is taking place at the bottom of a large dip in the terrain: the future apostle is being struck down and is protecting himself with his right hand from the ray of light from the sky. His companions have fallen back stupefied by the divine manifestation that has thrown their leader to the ground. Some of the hills are covered with woods and attractive undergrowth, and on one there stands a fortress. The fine blending of lines toward the horizon illustrates the exceptional skill and refined feeling of nuance also found in *The Return of the Prodigal Son*. An esplanade leading up to his father's sumptuous house is interspersed with groups of friends filling the space between the house and the main motif and serving as a human background to it. Lucas has chosen the moment when the prodigal son, emaciated, kneels holding out his hands in appeal and seeks the welcome that is not long in forthcoming. His face expresses nervous expectation and exhaustion. To the left in the yard of an imposing farm the fatted calf is being slain; to the right a peaceful country scene offers a contrast to the dramatic tension of the main incident: the cattle are being led out to pasture, a stretch of water leads to a village protected by large trees at the foot of a steep cliff. In the farmyard before the stretch of water, we see the episode in which the son, kneeling with the pigs, is ready to eat from their trough. Another outstandingly successful example of the technique of larger composition is the *Ecce Homo* (1510). The terraces and covered galleries of the patricians' houses line the public square. A curious crowd has gathered, their gestures and debate showing that they are passionately involved in the event that they are watching. In the foreground a more animated group is shouting hostile threats with raised fists. Christ, stripped, has just been led by a magistrate onto the tribunal reserved for habitual criminals, his head crowned with thorns, his body draped with the cloak of mockery, and its train held by the two executioners. Looking at this plate, which was immediately acclaimed, one cannot help comparing it to a medieval mystery play, and this is the same treatment adopted by Rembrandt in 1655 for his etching of the same subject. The work reveals a planned perspective, an acute sense of animation of the hundred or so watchers who make up the crowd, a cultivation of the picturesque in the costumes, the weapons, and the architecture. As the main theme with its four figures portrayed on a small scale is isolated in the middle ground, it is the clever balance of the masses of light and shade that gives the sprawling composition its unity. With Rembrandt and many others after him, one must admire the technical skill with the burin that achieved the silver and satin high lights of the plate.

An apparent concern with psychological analysis can be detected in the set of nine circular prints "The Passion of Christ, or the Round Passion" (1509). The savage joy, the unhealthy curiosity, the passionate hate are more successfully portrayed than the pain and the suffering of a comparatively un-moved Christ. The scenes of *Jesus on the Mount of Olives* and *The Carrying of the Cross* are again portrayed separately. Although they bear the monogram "L," Friedländer wonders if they are copies made by one of Lucas' pupils.

Delen divides Lucas' work before 1511 from that which ended with his stay in Antwerp and his meeting with Dürer. He even proposes to divide this period, considering that from 1515 the influence exerted by the engravings of Dürer becomes stronger. Too rigid a division would leave out of account the imagination of an artist, his variations, his returns to past memories, or his daring anticipations. It would be wrong to expect to be able to trace a regular development, for do not some of the works described above reveal the same quality, mastery, and character of those to come?

From 1512 onward Lucas concentrates on sets, beginning with "The Story of Joseph." Revealing a taste for the picturesque, concern with the construction of balanced, complete compositions, he portrays with animation characters who express in their poses or expressions their amazement or their curiosity. Potiphar's wife is seen as sensual and almost vulgar, Potiphar seems all-powerful, while his kneeling wife accuses poor Joseph; but the Pharaoh appears worn and tormented, as Joseph, in full control of himself, interprets his dreams. Jacob listening to his youngest son is completely absorbed in his story. To make his figures stand out in greater relief, Lucas creates a strong contrast of light and shade, as can be seen especially in the harmoniously drawn work in which Joseph in prison is interpreting the dreams of the cupbearer and the court baker.

A second set of seven larger woodcuts (about sixteen by eleven inches) has been dated 1513–14 and is known as the great series of woman, in which the pernicious domination of woman is illustrated in episodes taken chiefly from the Old Testament, but also from the heritage of traditions of Antiquity passed down through the Middle Ages. *Original Sin* takes place in a wooded landscape. Adam is seated near the tree around which the serpent is curled. Eve, seen in profile from the right, is approaching to offer an apple to her companion and is holding another in her left hand. In the background the angel is driving humanity's first parents out of the Garden of Eden through a monumental gate like that of a town. *Samson and Delilah* occupy the foreground of a composition that develops on four planes. Behind the screen of trees and rocks we witness the capture of the giant, and in the background can be seen a town and a range of mountains. *Solomon Worshiping the Idols* reveals his weakness in the evening of his life. Under the sway of his concubines, he turns away from the true God and builds monuments for the idols. A single concubine, elegantly dressed, is close to the sovereign, who is kneeling in front of the statue of a helmeted warrior holding an ox skull. A figure of love carrying a bow is portrayed above the niche. The onlookers are discussing the scene skeptically. *The Queen of Sheba before Solomon* is kneeling; her smile is enigmatic and emphasizes the guile of this princess. The two raised fingers of her right hand lead one to suppose that she is taking an oath to speak the truth; moreover she is placing her left hand in the muzzle of a lion. Solomon is seated on his throne, his scepter in his hand. The onlookers form a screen, concealing armed men whose pikes alone are visible. In front of them the court jester, with his cocked hat and bauble, stands a little apart. In the *Feast of Herodias* the beheading of St. John the Baptist can be seen through a window to the right. In a room in the palace Herod and Herodias are feasting with various companions, Salome is gliding forward in the foreground carrying the head of John the Baptist, while Herodias points a knife at the platter. The next two woodcuts are illustrations taken from the legacy of Antiquity, passed on through the Middle Ages, of the danger of a woman's power to the man who, for her charms, no longer fears even ridicule. One is *Virgil Suspended in a Basket*.

The daughter of the emperor Augustus, whom Virgil loves passionately without being in return the object of her favors, has agreed to pull him up to her room in the palace at night in a basket. But the impatient poet has talked indiscreetly of this rendezvous to his friends. The young woman takes her revenge by letting him spend the night suspended in midair in the basket. And this is how Virgil's friends find him when they come to mock him early the next morning. To the left of the composition a mother is moralizing on the incident to her young son. There is a Greek version, *Aristotle and Phyllis*, of this mocking of a man in love that was well known in the late Middle Ages in the form of the "Lay of Aristotle." Phyllis, also called Campaspe, was loved by the young Alexander. Aristotle tried to turn him away from this courtesan, but ended up being seduced by her himself. Taking leave of his senses, the philosopher agrees to go down on all fours and to carry astride him the object of his obsessive desire. Her hair flowing in the wind, Phyllis holds the reins in her left hand and in her right the whip.

A complete set of the great series of women is nowhere to be found; the Print Room of the National Library in Paris possesses the only copy of *Aristotle and Phyllis*. It is of rather crude design and reveals a certain inability to portray the nuances of transition from light to shade. The small series (about ten by seven inches) on the same theme, which comprises ten woodcuts dated 1517–18, is more decorative and is composed with a stronger sense of space and better portrayal of the atmosphere. It is inspired by the Old Testament, and in three instances again uses subjects treated in the great series. This does not at all mean that Lucas is repeating himself. The tree in *Original Sin* is more twisted and its branches more developed. Eve is lying casually against the trunk offering the apple to Adam, who is seated in a quite natural pose. The serpent is again holding an apple by its stalk in its mouth. The scene of the angel driving the sinners from the garden is taking place in the direction of a deep portal surmounted by a high gable that suggests a church. On the horizon appear barren mountains whose general shape can be made out only in silhouette. The characters of *Samson and Delilah* are more soberly portrayed than in its larger equivalent: Delilah is younger, more coquettish, a spiked mace replaces the sword, the stature of the giant is more clearly defined in the background scene. The three episodes of the story of Jael and Sisera are inspired by a few verses from the Book of Judges, although Lucas takes the liberty of transposing the locality from the biblical tent to a complex building. We watch the arrival of Sisera, the commander of Jabin's army, who has come to seek refuge in the village where lives Jael, the wife of Heber. Thirsty, he asks Jael for a drink, and she gives him what is no doubt a cup of milk, as the Bible tells that she opened a skin of milk and gave him to drink. But the soldier is exhausted; he enters a tent and falls into a deep sleep. Lucas has him stretch out in the middle of a courtyard so as to portray better his assassination. For Jael, seizing a tentpeg, drives it through Sisera's temple with a mallet, nailing his head to the ground. She hands him over dead to his enemies, led by Barac, who are approaching from the right; the murderess receives them with impassive indifference. *Solomon Worshiping the Idols* is a revised treatment of a theme already used five years previously. The figure of the devil carrying a flag and holding out an urn of flame occupies the dominant position, and this is emphasized by the raising of the effigy onto a monumental pedestal. An elegantly dressed woman is showing the false god to the old king, who is kneeling with his hands joined. There are only two witnesses who stand watching the scene. The four personages are placed in two parallel lines leading toward a mountainous landscape drawn with restraint but enlivened by a subtle play of line and high light. Jezebel had a decisive evil influence on her husband Ahab, the most ungodly of the kings of Israel, who built a temple to Baal in Samaria. In the woodcut *Jezebel and Her Husband, King Ahab*, she is portrayed giving orders to the king, who is lying in bed. Through the window can be seen the reception given to the prophet Elias, and through the door a scene of violence, no doubt ordered by the king who, under the influence of his wife, made war on the Syrians, seized Naboth's vineyard, and had the Lord's prophets put to death. *The Feast of Herodias* is the sixth example of the sometimes evil power of women illustrated in this smaller series. The beheading of St. John the Baptist is recalled in the top left corner. Into the banqueting hall Salome is carefully, and arrogantly, carrying the head of the martyr on a platter. Herod is feasting with the sensual Herodias. This woodcut does not have the quality of the one in the great series.

The "fourteen" Sibyls form a set of woodcuts representing half-length portraits of women. The twelve Sibyls are framed by the Synagogue and the Church, the first holds the tables of the law and a broken standard and is blindfolded; the second is wearing a crown with rosettes and holds the Cross with the Crucified and the book of the Apostles covered with the symbols of Christ and the Evangelists. The seven first sibyls carry attributes connected with episodes from Jesus' childhood, while the other five refer to scenes from the Passion and the Resurrection.

The effigies of the Saints, which illustrate so outstandingly the Missal of Utrecht Cathedral (1514) and the images of "The Twelve Kings of Israel" and "The Nine Knights," are series referred to later. There has been some discussion as to the authorship of these works. The name of Jacob Cornelisz. has often been brought up; so has that of Lucas. Whatever the case may be, the subject is a cavalcade, but the knights are more richly dressed and imaginary coats of arms adorn the cloths of the horses and the elephant. Lucas is influenced by current tradition in this. It is not the first time that he had designed a complicated coat of arms. In 1509 there was *The Standard of Jan Seversz.* and in the following year *The Coat of Arms of the City of Leyden*. He later portrayed more historical figures in the *Chronicle of Holland, Zeeland and Friesia* in 1517, from the *Duke Pepin of Brabant* to *The Emperor Charles V*, whom naturally he portrays as a young man.

Antique themes afford Lucas a pretext to evoke death. In *Pyramus and Thisbe* (1514) the protagonists are represented in an area of shade. Pyramus has killed himself by the fountain, which is crowned with a figure of love, as he believes Thisbe to have been eaten by a lioness. In brighter light the "attack by the lioness" is taking place in the background, but the animal only rips Thisbe's veil. Thisbe cannot survive the sight of the dead Pyramus and kills herself by throwing herself on the sword of the young Babylonian. The date of *The Suicide of Lucretia* is disputed. Beets insists that it was influenced by an engraving by Marcantonio Raimondi based on a drawing by Raphael that is preserved in the British Museum in London, the *Venus and Cupid*; in this case the work must have been produced after 1520. But whatever the truth, Lucretia's body seems supple despite its fleshy heaviness. Another fine print on the theme of death is the *Young Man with a Death's Head*, whom Van Mander identified without valid reason as the artist himself. It is simply the meditation of an elegant young man on a skull that he is discreetly displaying. The sixteenth century is known for its predilection for the *vanitas* and *memento mori*.

The subjects most frequently commissioned from Lucas are clearly those inspired by the Bible. *Abraham Kneeling before the Three Angels* retains a trace of the medieval spirit. *The Triumph of David* is untouched by the influence of the Italian Renaissance. Three young women have come before the victor who, unmoved, is carrying the head of Goliath in order to celebrate his triumph with music and song. The theme of *Solomon Worshiping the Idols* (1514) is taken up again, and once more Lucas varies his composition. The same applies to *Abraham Renouncing Hagar* (1516) in which one can detect a concern to create a more intimate scene: Hagar is wiping away a tear, Ishmael is tightly clutching his little basket of food. The position of the feet of the three protagonists is interesting: Abraham's are turned in the same direction as the gesture of his hand toward the repudiated woman whose painful hesitation is indicated by her right foot, which points toward Abraham, while Ishmael's seems already to move in the departure into the desert. The woodcuts, the *Sacrifice of Abraham* and *The Bloody Coat of Joseph Shown to Jacob*, are also treated with a tendency to convert the biblical episode into a genre scene. *The Triumph of Mordecai* (1515) is a remarkable technical achievement. The procession is advancing through the grateful crowd, the victor shows great dignity, Aman does not conceal his pride. To the rear of the landscape on top of the "Gibbet Hill" is erected the gallows with Aman hanging from it. *Esther before Ahasuerus* (1518) is no less brilliant. The favorite wife of the king of Persia, followed by two slightly frightened ladies-in-waiting, is humbling herself before the sovereign, asking him to dine with his minister Aman, for it is then that she is counting on obtaining a revocation of the cruel edict for the extermination of the Jews. Condescendingly, and even with good humor, the king is bending down toward Esther to indicate his agreement by touching her with his scepter, while Aman cannot contain his savage feelings. The closest onlookers, such as the two listening at the door, are discussing the moving scene with evident interest. The composition develops on four parallel planes achieved by the lessening of intensity of the blacks and the firmness of the strokes: first Esther and Ahasuerus, then the second plane with Aman and the two ladies-in-waiting, the screen of onlookers, the buildings of the palace with the two curious watchers on the right, and finally the landscape, subdivided still further in the evocation of the buildings in half-tones, and then the wooded, mountainous background that is overlooked by some lightly drawn walls.

The New Testament is recalled in images illustrating the three cycles of the life of Christ. In *The Annunciation*, dated about 1514, it is the effect of the Holy Ghost that Lucas seeks to emphasize by flooding the scene with light emanating from the halo surrounding Mary's head. The woodcut of 1519 represents Mary and the angel Gabriel more familiarly in conversation. *The Adoration of the Magi* (1513) is rather strangely composed. The foreground is divided into two groups. That on the left consisting of the Holy Family and the first Wise Man is more intimate and peaceful, while that on the right around the imposing Wise Man who is advancing with pomp is more agitated. Here, for the first time, Lucas tackles the problem of the moving figure, apart from his strivings to portray human beings who reveal their character through their gestures and expressions in the course of their conversation in pairs. In the woodcut *The Adoration of the Magi* (c. 1519) the engraver adopts the same style as in *The Annunciation*, for it is after all a series. *The Temptation of Jesus in the Desert* (1518) has as its main focal point the supreme serenity of Christ before the tempting suggestions of the old man with a claw foot wearing a pointed cowl and a cloak, one of the folds of which ends in the shape of a serpent. *The Prodigal Son*, the only known copy of which is in the Print Room of the National Library in Paris, is an inn scene composed of the young woman of easy virtue, the shameless, drunken old woman, the boy with a knowing look, and the fool who utters the telling reflection, "Wacht. hoet. varen. sal." ("Wait and see which way the wind turns"). While *Christ and the Samaritan Woman* is a picture with little soul, *Christ's Farewell to His Mother*, the only known copy of which is in the Albertina in Vienna, expresses with more sensitivity the painful feelings of Mary and her companions.

Five prints presented in the same general form constitute an incomplete series of a most moving

Passion that reflects some influence of Dürer: *The Crowning with Thorns*, the small *Ecce Homo*, *The Soldiers Giving Jesus to Drink* date from 1513–14, *Christ on the Cross between the Virgin and St. John* from 1516, *The Suffering Christ at the Tomb* from 1517. *The Carrying of the Cross* (1515) is really the moment when Christ stumbles in front of Veronica, who offers him her veil. *The Holy Visage held by St. Peter and St. Paul* (1517) is delicately engraved.

Looking through the *Treatise of Divine Love* by Bonaventura (1511), the *Missal of Utrecht Cathedral* (1514), and the *Garden of the Soul* (1515), one discovers, executed with much simpler lines and with deeper incisions in the wood, a great number of devotional images intended to illustrate various episodes from the life of Christ or the Virgin, and portraits of the saints who can be identified not only by the accompanying text, but also by the attributes that characterize them. To this series can be added *St. Dominic, St. Francis of Assisi receiving the Stigmata*, and *St. Gerard*. Sometimes the artist, undertaking a special commission, carves on wood or engraves on copper. *The Virgin and the Child, The Virgin with a Rosary*, which is only to be found in the British Museum in London, *St. Peter*, the only copy of which is in the Metropolitan Museum in New York, are all part of the same set of woodcuts. *The Virgin with the Child Jesus in a Niche* (c. 1518), like *The Abduction of St. Mary Magdalen* (1518), which are both the same size, reveal a quest for elegance not only in the clothes but in the figures. In both Lucas portrays a tall, slim woman resting on the crescent of a moon or on clouds, her body much less plump than usual with him, her head standing out against an enormous halo of bright light. One can measure the considerable progress made by Lucas between the more traditional, heavier *Virgin and the Child Jesus in Glory* (c. 1512) and these elegant pictures. *The Virgin with the Child Jesus, Seated at the Foot of a Tree* (1514), a plate inspired by an engraving by Dürer in 1511, is heavily built, but the fullness given to the cloak, which fills the whole of the lower part of the composition, gives her an impression of noble ease. Finally, and this is an undeniable link, the Madonna in *St. Anne, the Virgin, and the Child Jesus* (1516) already achieves indisputable elegance. Lucas represents "The Four Evangelists" (1518) in half-length portraits at their desks in the silence of a tightly enclosed space. They are tensely concentrating in an effort to comprehend their inspiration. *St. Jerome in the Desert*, on the other hand, is presented either absorbed in his reading (1513) or doing penance (1516), but in both instances in the foreground of a landscape. It is true, however, that these two works are prior to the period when the new trends made it fashionable to portray saints in their studies.

This period so rich in experiment and in success also contains several large plates representing crowded scenes that are sequels to *The Conversion of St. Paul* (1509) and the *Ecce Homo* of 1510. One is *Calvary* (1517), a suberb composition that has inspired a good number of Lucas' successors. The first printing is known to be very rare and consequently is much sought after; the date appears on it with its figures in the reverse order, which is corrected in the second version. A large crowd is portrayed in motley, episodic groups of men who are for the most part indifferent witnesses of the drama being enacted on Golgotha. The artist fills the plate with anecdotal scenes, with characters involved in their own private conversations. In places, gestures and poses direct one's attention to the Crucified; a group of poor pilgrims in the lower right-hand corner are looking toward the scene of suffering and show feelings of understanding and compassion. The apparently scattered crowd is in fact perfectly planned and organized. They describe large ellipses encircling Golgotha, which is defined against the light filtering through the shaded sky and the dazzling light dissolving the outlines of the landscape to the right. The three crosses stand out against the dark clouds with an air of tragedy. The drama is drawing to its close: the wicked one has just been crucified, the spear has pierced the side of Jesus, the Virgin is fainting. Lucas contrasts the indifference of the crowd with the concentrated attention of the faithful at the foot of the Cross, who suffer with the Tortured Christ.

Another of this series is *The Dance of Magdalen* (1519), a social gathering in a grove. To the right three elegant couples are exchanging confidences; a poet, his head crowned with a garland, sits uninterested beside them. On the other side a soldier is stretched out beside his lady, while a fool is hailing, perhaps with malicious intent, a group emerging from the wood. Two musicians are about to strike up a slow tempo to which the haloed Magdalen and her gallant are preparing to dance. Everything seems peaceful and a little cold in this dignified genre scene that avoids all vulgarity. The engraver's strokes are rather wide and deep, forming a clear contrast to the soft light dominating the background scene, in which we see Magdalen taking part in a hunt on horseback. The open clearing into which she is riding is vast and is surrounded by sparse clumps of trees; in the background there rises majestically the rocky mass where one can make out the cave sheltering the penitent, about to be carried up by four angels to hear the celestial concert.

Finally there is *The Ship of St. Reynuyt, or the Ship of Mismanagement* (c. 1520), a group of eight wood blocks creating an animated, satirical tableau swarming with people whose actions illustrate man's evil appetites.

No doubt Lucas' prolonged stay in Antwerp, his frequenting of the offices of engravers and editors, his meeting with Dürer, the journey with Jean Gossart, each had its influence on his ever alert mind and left its mark on his creations. His curiosity about everything connected with the engraver's art led him to experiment. He executed seven known prints by etching, which he sometimes retouched with the burin to achieve the desired effect. *The Abduction of St. Mary Magdalen* is the first example, bearing the date 1518 in reverse. Then there are the six works produced in 1520: *The Murder of Abel, David in Prayer, St. Catherine of Alexandria, The Fool Kissing a Woman, The Bohemians,* or *Huilenspiegel,* a rare engraving which had such success that Hondius reissued it in 1644. It portrays the journey of two "Bohemians" (strolling players) carrying children. Finally there is the *Portrait of the Emperor Maximilian I,* an exact copy of the woodcut executed by Dürer in 1519. The biting of the acid no doubt enabled the artist to obtain more easily the effect of halftones. But it is noticeable that Lucas has used the burin to retouch especially the more expressive areas such as the face.

Caricature was in fashion in Antwerp. Lucas had already introduced one or two distorted faces into his earlier compositions but he was to use them more frequently, either because he came to attach more importance to them or because he handled subjects calling for more grotesque and misshapen personages: the enemies of Christ in the Passion, the vulgar characters in the scenes of love or daily life. Does he portray an old man or an *Old Woman with a Bunch of Grapes* as the traditional title would indicate? On the one hand, the drinker's nose given to the personage is pointed out; on the other, it is felt that the figure has the hands of a woman. Anyway, in this study of an ugly face, like that in *The Fool Kissing a Woman*, this head calls to mind the style popularized by the workshop of Quentin Massys. There are more caricatured figures in *The Crowning with Thorns* (1519). The portrayal of the coarse features of uncouth peasants becomes the indispensable ingredient of burlesque subjects like the scene at *The Dentist* (1523), where the poor patient suffers not only from the treatment he is undergoing, but unbeknown to him, is being duped by an artful woman who is emptying his purse. This last indignity is spared the man whose stone of madness the surgeon is attempting to remove by bleeding him behind the ear in *The Surgeon and the Peasant* (1524). *The Musicians* (1524) are touching in their aging vulgarity; the man is struggling to tune his lute, while his toothless companion waits to begin playing her violin. In *The Murder of Abel* (1524) Cain is portrayed as a huge ruffian. Adam is scarcely more distinguished in *Original Sin* (1519).

The new trends leave their mark on the biblical and religious themes. Although the influence of Dürer is even more clearly to be detected, as in "The Small Passion" (1521), *The Virgin and the Child Jesus in Glory*, and *The Virgin and the Child Jesus, Seated at the Foot of a Tree with Two Adoring Angels* (1523), one must also underline the efforts of Lucas to portray bodies seen from an angle, hunched up, or in plunging perspective, as can be observed in *The Descent from the Cross* and *The Resurrection* (1521), or *The Murder of Abel* (1524). *St. Jerome in his Study* (1521) is more a study of the rather complicated pose of the cardinal's body than a profound meditation on the vanities of the world and death. In *St. Anthony the Hermit*, St. Anthony's bearing is emphasized more than his hermit's characteristics. It is the muscular effort with its effects on the dynamics of the body that Lucas expresses above all in *Lamech and Cain* (1524), and he places the guard stringing his bow well in the foreground. Physical force almost entirely dominates *St. Christopher Carrying the Child Jesus*. The intense religious feeling gives way to a more relaxed, even more familiar and sentimental mood. For *The Meeting of Anne and Joachim* (1520), like *The Visitation* (1520), serves as a pretext for effusive portrayals. *The Appearance of Christ as a Gardener to St. Mary Magdalen* (1519) illuminates the sweetness of the woman who was forbidden to touch the Saviour. The treatment of the religious theme is very close to that of genre. The same tenderness is found in *The Promenade* (1520) and in the *Young Couple Seated in a Landscape* (1520). The young woman accepting the goblet offered by her fiancé seems so much more elegant than *The Young Woman at the Spinning Wheel*, though admittedly this woodcut dates from about 1513. The same delicacy is also found in the work that has wrongly been entitled *Self-Portrait of the Artist*, an etching bearing Lucas' monogram, the date 1525, and an identifying inscription that is, however, considered to be a print from the seventeenth century.

Virgil Suspended in a Basket is a new version as an engraving of a subject treated as a woodcut in 1513–14. The comparison of the two compositions is extremely interesting and shows how the artist in 1525 is more engrossed in the manner of portrayal than in the subject itself. As a balance to the crowd of onlookers and the basket in full view carrying the pitiful Virgil, the unfortunate lover, Lucas now adds a spacious scene animated by groups of people extending through several planes. These are the eight figures ranged to the right in varied poses and costumes that reveal their social rank. The whole group stands out in high relief from the screen of a sober Renaissance building. Three children—putti in shifts—are in the foreground of a deep space interrupted by two men near a low wall and then three others more lightly sketched. This finally takes one up to the palace, which is portrayed with delicate strokes and high lights. Virgil is suspended halfway up the wall and is mocked in this pitiful plight from a window by the daughter of Augustus and from the ground by a group of Romans.

Lucas' last three active years were 1527–30.

He added several more woodcuts illustrating the Bible, such as *The Baptism of Christ* with St. John seated, and *St. Peter on a Globe before a Niche*. He devoted part of his time in 1527–28 to creating decorative motifs in a new style, elegant ornaments composed, in among twining branches, of sphinxes, tritons, sirens, dolphins, mythological animals, and warriors' heads in circular frames. The putti and children play an important part in them, just as the winged genii animated the medallions that he engraved ten years earlier.

It was on the nude figure that he focused his attention during this period, when in 1526–27 he also painted his great *Last Judgment*. "The Story of the First Couple" (1529), starting with *The Creation of Eve* through to the pathetic *The Lamentation of Adam and Eve over the Body of Abel*, is a set of six engravings inspired by Marcantonio Raimondi, dominated by nude figures in free, sometimes violent movement, as in *The Murder of Abel*. Although the *Original Sin* of 1529 is conceived in the traditional mood, the wider plate of the same subject (1530) is impregnated with the new spirit of the Renaissance: it is a more carefully planned composition with Adam seated in a grove, his head seen in profile from the left. He is stretching out his right hand to take the apple offered by a more agitated but attractive Eve. A gentle light suffuses the background, softening the outlines of the trees that enclose the open space. In *Venus and Cupid* (1528) the goddess is portrayed in a pose rather similar to that of Adam; her delicate body is finely highlighted. The text in French inscribed on the decorative streamer, "Venus the most beautiful goddess of love," seems to prove that Lucas was anxious to assure a wide distribution for his work. *Mars, Venus, and Cupid* (1530) is more dependent on Italian models; the line is more geometric, the strokes wider and crossing, and the form, though the figures are still buxom and amply fleshed, triumphs over the subtle effects of light and shade. The same applies to *Lot and His Daughters* (1530) and

25

"The Theological and Cardinal Virtues" (1530). The latter are in every case real naked goddesses as Raimondi would have portrayed them. They are in seven different poses, as are the putti coming to crown the symbolic figures that can be identified by their attributes and the inscription of their titles in Roman capitals.

Lucas' engraving developed over a period of twenty-five years. Living in a pivotal age between the end of the Middle Ages, which was exhausting itself in Mannerist formulae, and the beginning of the Renaissance, obsessed by ideals, classical beauty, and seeking noble proportions, true perspective, and poised equilibrium, the master of Leyden was exposed to different artistic currents and absorbed varied influences. He did not limit himself to a faded, facile Mannerism but imposed on himself a discipline of strict observation that enabled him to discover the living reality of men who act and who know passion. He gives renewed life to the problems discussed in all the workshops. The dynamics of the human figure, the giving of depth to scenes in which the personages of a theme should be harmoniously integrated, these were the objects of his study. The engravings of Albrecht Dürer encouraged him in this direction as did the Italian prints, among them those of Marcantonio Raimondi. It was through this intermediary that Lucas became acquainted with the solutions worked out by the Italian masters. His friendly relations with Jean Gossart gave him the opportunity to discuss these questions. Dying at a very early age, Lucas did not have the chance to show strongly his personal reactions to the lessons that he was doing his utmost to incorporate in the works of his last years. A precocious artist, extremely sensitive, receptive while at the same time retaining his originality, he was unable to integrate the new Italian influence into his customary personal style. His study of proportion, his technical experiments leading him to use deeper strokes and wider, crossing hachures, would only have increased his capabilities. Similarly his experiments in etching in 1518–20 only strengthened his concern to achieve more delicate, subtler, and more silvery effects of light to animate the deep spaces that serve as a framework to his compositions and to lighten his woodcuts by the opposition of black and white surfaces. The integrity of his technique is clear; one has only to consider his prints or his independent and illustrative woodcuts. A connoisseur like Rembrandt attached the highest importance to this technical aspect. Van Mander reports significant evidence of this. "I have learnt, and his daughter vouched for it, that he burnt great heaps of proofs that were imperfectly printed."

The technique of engraving impassioned Lucas, an indefatigable worker, and every subject interested him. Of universal outlook, he tackled with equal success the religious images of the Old and New Testaments, mythological themes, subjects from Antiquity from which the Middle Ages had drawn morals, and symbolic figures. He treated traditional iconography with respect, but entertained innovations imposed by the composition or introduced to enliven a theme. For it is man who was the object of the concentrated attention of the penetrating observer that was Lucas. He follows man at work or at rest, in conversation, in his calculated actions, or in his hours of relaxation. Humble peasants, picturesque vagabonds, anxious men of power, their arrogant courtiers and deceivers, all are evoked in their turn, in action and at peace, in a setting of the architecture of the period or in a landscape radiant with light, which filters through the trees or floods the valleys and meadows. Lucas van Leyden celebrated the daily life of his contemporaries, and in that was one of the initiators of this tendency so characteristic of Dutch art. But he communed with what is most profound in man, and by his remarkable understanding of the motives and behavior of the human being, he dominates his school and stands isolated from his contemporaries as does Rembrandt in the seventeenth century, belonging instead to the individuals of genius who honor and guide humanity.

BIBLIOGRAPHICAL NOTES

There are numerous works devoted to Lucas van Leyden. A list of many of them appears in the bibliography compiled by H. van HALL, *Repertorium voor de geschiedenis der Nederlandsche schilder- en graveerkunst sedert het begin der 12de eeuw tot het eind van 1946* (The Hague, 1936–49). Among monographs on the painter, draftsman, and engraver, we cite: N. BEETS, *Lucas de Leyden* (Paris and Brussels, 1913); G. J. HOOGEWERFF, *De Noord-Nederlandsche schilderkunst*, vol. III (The Hague, 1939); M. J. FRIEDLÄNDER, *Lucas van Leyden*, edited by Fr. WINKLER (Berlin, 1963). Basic works relative to the engravings of Lucas van Leyden (chronology, technique, and style) are: A. BARTSCH, *Le Peintre-graveur*, vol. VII (Vienna, 1808); Th. VOLBEHR, *Lucas van Leyden, Verzeichnis seiner Kupferstich, Radierungen und Holzschnitte* (Hamburg, 1888); M. J. FRIEDLÄNDER, *Lucas van Leyden (Meister der Graphik, XIII)* (Leipzig, 1924); F. W. H. HOLLSTEIN, *Dutch and Flemish Etchings, Engravings, and Woodcuts*, vol. X (Amsterdam, n.d.). Numerous articles have been published by Fr. DUELBERG and Campbell DODGSON, especially the latter's *Beschreibendes Verzeichnis der Buchillustrationen Lucas van Leydens* in *Repertorium für Kunstwissenschaft*, vol. XXIII (1910), pp. 143–53. Recent exhibitions devoted to the works of Lucas van Leyden should be mentioned, as their catalogues are well documented: *Lucas van Leyden en tijdgenoten*, Rotterdam, Boymans Museum, December, 1952; *Exposition Lucas de Leyde, Gravures* (catalogue edited by Fr. Lugt), Paris, Institut Néerlandais, April 14–30, 1959; *Mostra delle incisioni di Luca di Leida* (catalogue edited by M. FOSSI TODOROW), Florence, Gabinetto dei Disegni e delle Stampe degli Uffizi, 1963.

PHOTOGRAPHICAL SOURCES

All photographs have been supplied by the Rijksmuseum, Amsterdam, except for the following:
Albertina, Vienna: 10, 210
Bibliothèque Nationale, Paris: 194, 214
Bisschoppelijk Museum, Haarlem: 256, 258, 260–73, 275–84, 286–90, 292, 294–311
British Museum, London: 22, 190, 191, 209, 223, 257, 291, 312, 313, 315, 316, 318
Gabinetto dei Disegni e delle Stampe degli Uffizi, Florence: 59, 60
Institut Néerlandais, Paris (Collection F. Lugt): 36, 96, 173
Koninklijke Bibliotheek, The Hague: 259, 274, 285, 293
Kunstsammlungen der Veste, Coburg: 226–29, 232, 233
Metropolitan Museum of Art, New York (Rogers Fund, 1918): 216
Musées Nationaux, Paris: 187
Museum Boymans-van Beuningen, Rotterdam: 15, 20, 32–34, 73, 74, 92, 95, 110, 111, 115, 177, 250–52
National Gallery of Art, Washington, D.C. (Rosenwald Collection): 49
Walter Steinkopf, Berlin: 314, 317
Wolter, Düsseldorf: 37

PLATES

4

6

7

9

10

11

12

13

14

15

16

17

18

19

20

21

22

1409

23

1409

24

25

26

1409

27

28

1409

29

1409

30

31

32

34

33

35

36

37

38

39

40

41

42

43

44

45

46

47

48

49

50

51

52

53

54

55

56

57

58

59

60

61

62

63

64

65

66

67

68

69

70

71

72

73

74

75

76

77

79

80

81

82

83

84

85

86

87

88

89

90

91

92

95

96

97

98

99

100

103

104

102

105

106

107

108

109

110

111

112

113

114

115

116

117

1519 L

119

120

121

122

123

124

125

126

127

128

129

130

131

132

133

134

135

136

137

138

139

140

141

142

143

144

145

146

147

148

149

150

151

152

153

154

155

156

Effigies lucæ leidensis, propria manu incidere.

157

158

159

160

161

162

VENVS LA TRESBELLE DEESSE DAMOVRS

1528
L

163

164

165

166

167

168

169

171

172

1530   L

174

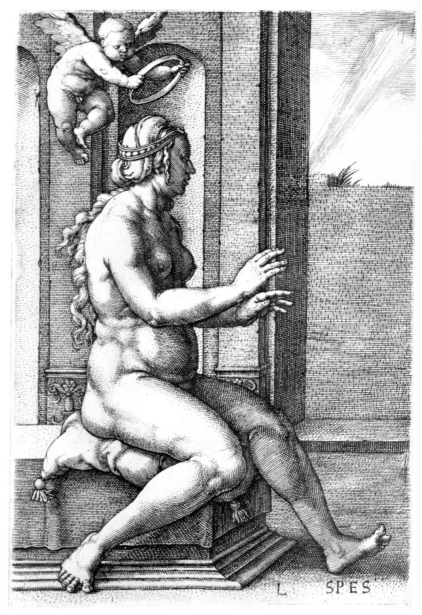

L FIDES

L SPES

175

176

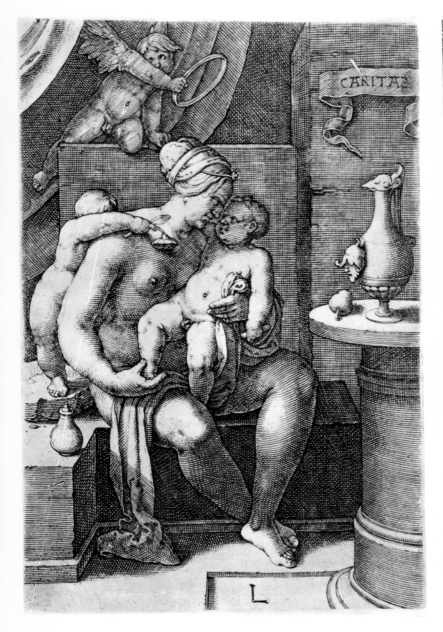

177

178

IVSTICIA·

VORTITVDO

179

180

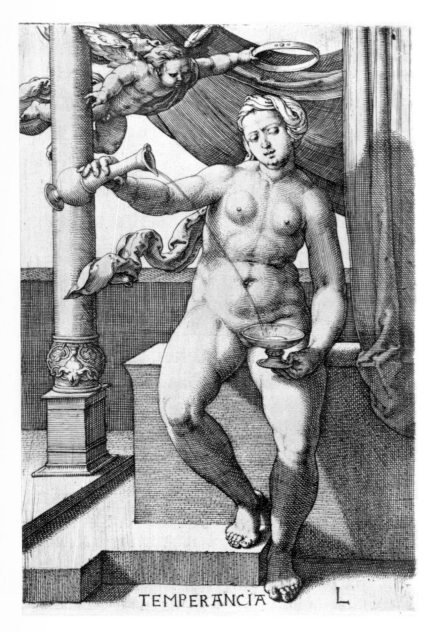

TEMPERANCIA   L

181

182

183

184

185

186

187

195

196

197

198

201

202

203

211

212

213

215

216

217

218

221

222

224

226

227

228

229

230

231

232

233

234

235

236

237

238

239

240

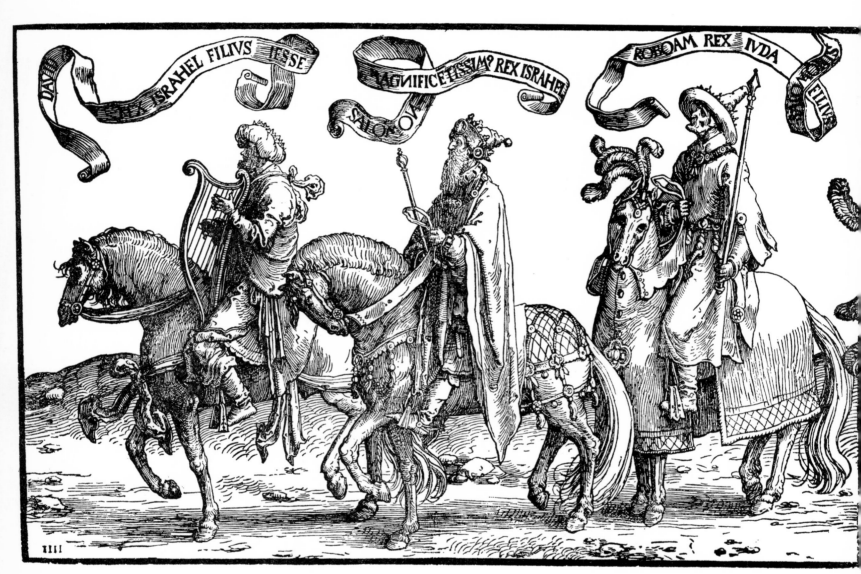

242

243

244

245

ROBOAM REX IVDA SALOMONIS FILIVS

ROBOAM · REX IVDA

ASA FILIVS ABIA REX IVDA

247

NATHAN FILIVS OSI...R...IVDA

HECTOR · TROIANS   ALEXANDER   MACEDO   IVLIVS·CAESAR

250

IOSVE · REX · N   DAVID REX ISRAHEL   IVDAS MACHABEVS

251

ALEXANDER MACED[O]

253

GODEFRIDVS BILLONIVS

255

256

257

258   259   260   261   262   263   264

265   266   267   268   269   270   271

272   273   274   275   276   277   278

279   280   281   282   283   284   285

286

288

287

289

290

INRI

291

292   293

294   295   296   297

298

299   *300*

301   *302*   *303*   *304*

305   *306*

307

308

309

310

311

312

313

314

315

316

317

318

Pieter Bruegel
the Elder

The school of painting and engraving of the southern Netherlands boasts one of the most original masters of the sixteenth century—Pieter Bruegel the Elder. It is through his arresting personality and inquisitive mind that he stands out from his fellow artists, as does El Greco among Spanish painters, and it is these qualities that his contemporaries and following generations looked for in his brilliant paintings and drawings, or his meticulously composed engravings.

While the Flemish primitives were models for their time, the ideal of their successors in the sixteenth century was to become disciples of the Italian Renaissance masters. The colorists were more interested in form, sometimes quite complicated form, than in the genres and themes of allegory and Antiquity, but they did not interpret them in the same way as their southern rivals.

Bruegel was not unaware of Italy, which he came to know well, nor was he unaffected by the humanism that he encountered among his scholarly friends, but he never denied his artistic origins nor abandoned the fine technical traditions on which was based the greatness of the Flemish School. It is his faithfulness to these refined techniques that shows him to be a closer disciple of the masters of the fifteenth century than were Bernard van Orley or especially Jean Gossart, although they belonged to the preceding generation. Above all he is faithful to the traditional source of inspiration: man — his behavior, his soul, his heart. He pays less attention to man's physical aspect, especially when judged by academic criteria rather than by direct observation of the reality of everyday life. In fact Bruegel is linked with the fifteenth century through Hieronymus Bosch and the church-stall carvers, while at the same time participating fully, but with individuality, in the spirit of his own period. It is this combination that assured his success. Collectors fought over his paintings, drawings, and engravings. His work was copied, reissued; it served as inspiration for several centuries not only in his native country, but also in Holland, France, and Italy. But these are mere reflections of his talent.

It is important to give a brief account of the short life of this surprising man, for there are dates that stand out as landmarks and events that explain aspects of his art.

Karel van Mander is almost the sole biographical source, and he must be consulted with caution. He devotes a short paragraph of his *Book of the Painters* (1604) to Bruegel, whose work is so alien to him, an academic, a Mannerist.

The historian reports that Bruegel was born in the district of Breda, in a village of central Brabant, "whose name he adopted and passed down to his descendants." Van Mander is not alone in making the absurd assumption that one can determine a person's birthplace by his name. Family names had existed since the fourteenth century. Bruegel is said to be the son of a peasant, born around 1530; he died in 1569 at the age of forty. He settled in the important Brabantine city of Antwerp and was registered there with the St. Luke Guild of painters. The register of the "Liggeren" refers to him as "son of Bruegel."

Van Mander does not give a precise date to his journey to Italy, but he insists that "Bruegel painted a number of landscapes so faithful to nature that it could be said that in crossing the Alps he had swallowed mountains and rocks to vomit them forth on his return onto wood and canvas." His itinerary can be traced from these works. He approached the Alps through the upper Rhone Valley, which he recalls in the set "Twelve Large Landscapes." Evidence of a stay in Rome is his drawing *Ripa Grande*. He visited Tivoli, traveled to Naples, whose harbor he illustrates (Rome, Galleria Doria), and pushed on down to Sicily, since he sites the *Naval Combat in the Straits of Messina* with topographical accuracy. The main object of this journey, which he must have undertaken between 1551, the date of his registration in Antwerp, and 1553, the start of his collaboration with Jerome Cock, was to see the buildings and landscapes of Italy itself rather than make a pilgrimage to the masterpieces of Antiquity and the Renaissance.

Van Mander, always partial to gossip, emphasizes a more frivolous aspect of the young artist, and we can leave him the responsibility of having originated this view of Pieter Bruegel. "A merchant, Hans Franckert by name, commissioned numerous paintings from him. He was an excellent man much attached to the painter. Franckert and Bruegel enjoyed frequenting village festivities and marriages.... In Antwerp he lived on marital terms with a servant girl, whom he would have made his wife had she not been an incorrigible liar. He made an agreement with her whereby he was to mark all her lies on a fair-sized tally-stick that he had selected. If the tally was completed the marriage was to be abandoned, and this was what happened before very long." Whatever the truth of the matter, 1553 marked the start of Bruegel's work in the service of Jerome Cock, the able publisher of the famous house known as "The Four Winds." Bruegel's stay in Antwerp ended in 1563, the year of his marriage to Mayken Coecke, the daughter of the scholarly painter Pierre Coecke, who died in Brussels in 1550. If one is to believe Van Mander, Bruegel had "often carried in his arms" the daughter of the painter whom he calls—and one wonders why—"the master of the young painter." His future mother-in-law made it a condition of the marriage that the suitor should come to live in Brussels "to detach him from his former liaison." The couple lived in the picturesque and busy Rue Haute. Seven years later, in 1569, Bruegel died. He was buried in his parish church, Notre-Dame-de-la-Chapelle, where his body still lies in the southern side-aisle. A friend, Abraham Ortelius, a geographer of high repute, composed an epitaph included in his *Album amicorum*, which is preserved at Pembroke College, Cambridge. This pompous text begins with the words, "Petrum Brugelium pictorem fuisse sui seculi absolutissimum, nemo nisi invidus, emulus aut eius artis ignarus, umquam negabit. Sed quod nobis media etatis flore abreptus sit..."

Bruegel signed a good number of paintings, especially between 1557 and 1569, and there are also some drawings extant from between 1551 and 1557. At the present time, until a thorough scientific study can be made, the final and most important criterion in separating the genuine works of the master from the numerous copies and interpretations is that of quality.

All that one can say of the engravings bearing Bruegel's signature is that they are listed from 1553 and were still being published long after his death. René van Bastelaer drew up a list in 1908 that has been accepted as the basic catalogue of Bruegel's engravings. This learned author adopts a consecutive numbering that reaches 278 and covers not only the contemporary prints of the artist but also the reprints, variations, copies, and occasionally even nineteenth-century interpretations.

One must be selective. Only one print is extant that can be identified as actually being Bruegel's own work, *Landscape with Hare Shooting*. He signed it and dated it 1566. It is an original etching retouched with the burin and was immediately produced and distributed by Jerome Cock. With magnificent strokes, though some of the burin work is less expert, with a luminous quality and delicate touch, the artist portrays a vast landscape dominating the hunting scene in the foreground, which appears as merely episodic, although it has undeniable picturesque charm.

Bruegel made the drawings, which the engravers reproduced on copper, and in one instance on wood, for *The Masquerade of Ourson and Valentin*, which the printsellers edited and distributed. Now, despite the number of interpreters and the variety of their work, one is struck by the close relationship that exists among the prints originating from Bruegel's pen and pencil. From this one must conclude that his preparatory drawings were extremely detailed. This is borne out by one of the most knowledgeable experts on the subject, Louis Lebeer, who writes that Bruegel's drawings could almost have served as "drawn engravings" that were easily transposable, stroke for stroke, onto metal. In his composition Bruegel foresees the effects to be achieved in the engraving and leaves no freedom to the engravers, whose job is to reproduce rather than interpret his work. His engraved work stands out, as do all his drawings that have not been engraved, through the restraint and economy of means, through the expressive power of line. While the painter sees his subjects as patches of color subject to the subtle play of brilliant, immaterial light, the draftsman gives maximum importance to line that surrounds and silhouettes human, animal, or vegetable forms, evokes the varied aspects of landscapes, and underlines temperament and passion· This restraint, which Laran qualifies as "laconic incisiveness," enables him to establish a hierarchy of planes, to express the density of mass and the roundness of form. Drawings signed and dated by Bruegel, from which engravings were made, are carefully preserved in Amsterdam, Berlin, Brussels, Florence, Hamburg, London, Oxford, Paris, Rotterdam, and Vienna, in the Von Hirsch collection in Basel and the Lugt collection at the Netherlands Institute in Paris. Comparison of these with the corresponding prints bears out the truth of the above observations. Sometimes the engravings have a few hatchings made of short strokes; these are the work of interpreters attempting to achieve relatively facile effects more quickly .

Like Holbein, who worked for Frobenius in Basel, Bruegel chose to collaborate from 1553 onward with Jerome Cock of Antwerp. On his return from Italy in 1548, Cock opened a shop near the Nouvelle-Bourse on the corner of the Courte-Rue-Neuve and the Sainte-Catherine rampart. He gave it a proud name, Aux Quatre Vents (The Four Winds), which is a true indication of the variety of his talents. In fact its founder was a painter, draftsman, engraver, rhetorician, and above all, an art dealer, who made good use of lessons learned in Italy, as well as his close relations with the humanists of the period. As a publisher of prints he succeeded in his aim of spreading knowledge of Rome, with its buildings, its ancient monuments, the Italian landscape, and above all, the greatest artistic creations of the Renaissance masters. In order to achieve this, he engaged a remarkable team of engravers who spread the influence of Italian art in all its forms throughout the Low Countries. The Antwerp masters were joined by engravers from the north, as well as the Mantuan, Giorgio Ghisi. Besides these artists, whose work was exceptionally wide in its scope, there was a draftsman, Pieter Bruegel, who supplied original work. The reputation of Jerome Cock's office surpassed that of "The Golden Compass," which was later run by Christopher Plantin and his son-in-law, Jean Moretus.

Jerome Cock received from Bruegel nearly 135 drawings that he had engraved by various contributors, thus forming an extraordinary collection of plates that usually bear his name as publisher, or if not, his sign. Pierre van der Heyden, also called A Merica or Myricinus, a master in Antwerp in 1557, was one of the most frequent reproducers of Bruegel's drawings. Frans Huys should also be mentioned. On occasion Jerome Bos, Barthélemy de Mumpere, and others executed engravings from his original drawings. Nor must one omit Jerome Cock himself, whose burin work was particularly skillful.

Cock was not the sole distributor of Bruegel's work. On his death, which occurred a year after Bruegel's (1570), dealers competed for the plates and the unpublished drawings of Bruegel, for their customers still wanted his work. On this score, archives of the Antwerp Painters' Guild contain a significant reference. It is reported that Bruegel's widow kept several copper plates engraved from her husband's work in order to do business with them. Philippe Galle set up as a publisher in Antwerp in 1571 and acquired an important collection of plates which he reissued. His son Theodore and his grandson Jean, as well as Adrien Collaert, the son-in-law of Philippe Galle, exploited this stock right up to the third quarter of the seventeenth century. Jerome Wierix continued the tradition; Georges Hoefnagel, Corneille van Thienen, Martin van den Enden, all occasionally published some of his plates.

The sale of Bruegel's prints remained active; dealers had his unpublished drawings engraved. *Jesus and the Adulteress*, drawn in 1565, was published simultaneously by Pierre Perret and Pierre Jode in 1579 and later by Nicolas Visscher; in 1571 Philippe Galle published *Jesus and His Disciples on the Road to Emmaus*; the five plates making up the set "The Pilgrimage of the Epileptics to the Church of St. John at Molenbeek" was not issued until 1642. Artists were commissioned to complete unfinished series: Hans Bol added *Autumn* and *Winter* to Bruegel's *Spring* and *Summer* drawn in 1565 and 1568, with Jerome Cock publishing "The Four Seasons" in 1570; Adrien Brouwer completed the set, "Heads of Peasants," only one plate of which bears the mention "P. Bruegel inventor." Above all they assured successive editions that even during Bruegel's lifetime were gaining considerable momentum.

There are numerous states of Bruegel's engravings. Four versions of one composition are quite usual; *The Witch of Malleghem* has five. The different versions are marked by, for example, the addition of minor personages, of various lines, or by the reduction of the size, the valuable evidence of the names of the engravers and successive publishers, the name "Bruegel inventor" sometimes appearing only on later versions, by interpretative texts on the subjects in Latin, Flemish, or French, and finally by the figures or letters thereon. All of this reveals how anxious publishers were not only to publish sets composed by Bruegel, but also to make up albums of his work, as is illustrated by the set of "Small Landscapes of Brabant and Campine." These compositions were published several times in different sets. The first state, published by Jerome Cock, consists of two sets, the first published in 1559 under the title *"Multifariarum casularum ruriumque lineamenta curiosa ad vivum expressa,"* the second in 1561 under another title, *"Proediorum villarum et rusticorum icones elengantissimae* [sic] *ad vivum in aere deformatae libro secundo."* Jerome Cock had a second version printed in 1561, an edition in which he groups together the two sets and reduces the size of some of the plates. Theodore Galle issued a third edition in 1601 without the slightest alteration to the landscapes; the set bears a new title, *"Regiones et villae rusticae ducatus potissimum Brabantiae a Cornelio Curtio in pictorum gratiam artificiose depictae, a Theodoro Gallaeo excusae et in lucem editae. Antwerpiae, MDCI."* Jean Galle produced a fourth edition changing the order of the plates, which he gives a new numbering. This is the third version, for there are alterations; he adds more personages, new scenes of work in the fields, small details like smoke or sections of wall. It includes additional plates composed by Bol and Van der Borght. There follows a fifth edition, again with some retouching, constituting a fourth version. A final edition reduced in size was issued by Claes Jansz. or Nicolas Visscher in Amsterdam in 1612, *"Regiunculae et villae aliquot ducatus Brabantiae a P. Breugelis delineatae et in pictorum gratiam, a Nicolao Joannis Piscatore excusae et in lucem editae. Amsterdami 1617."* This is the first time that Pieter Bruegel's name appears, replacing that of Corneille Cort, which had adventurously been put forward by the publishers Theodore and Jean Galle thirty years after his death. Some critics have contested the identification proposed by Nicolas Visscher, who gladly misuses the names of great artists. But in the present instance there is a similarity between the engravings of 1612 and what Bruegel called his *"ad vivum"* drawings, which date from 1559 to 1561; some additions of minor personages can be attributed to Corneille Cort.

Nicolas Visscher and Hendrik Hondius were two of the most important promoters of Bruegel's work in the seventeenth century, following in the tradition of men like Cock, Galle, and Wierix. But there were also others such as Harmen Adolfsz. of Haarlem, and Paul de la Houve of the Louvre in Paris.

These prints were executed from Bruegel's drawings. In the seventeenth century Lucas Vosterman made an engraving based on a drawing by Rubens, but was himself inspired by a drawing by Bruegel, *The Brawl of the Peasants.* It was more from a picture by Bruegel belonging to Rubens than from Rubens' drawing in the Mariette collection that Vosterman executed the etching entitled *The Yawning Peasant.* In both these cases they are interpretative engravings aimed at achieving pictorial effects of light and shade, and this applies to all succeeding prints based on paintings. It is useless to dwell on these, for they do not reveal Bruegel's original drawing, but merely emphasize the success of his panels and canvases. This is not the case in the engravings of the skilled burinist Philippe Galle, who in 1574 was inspired by a grisaille painted by Bruegel about 1564 at the request of his friend Abraham Ortelius, *The Death of the Virgin*, which was previously in Rubens' collection but is now at the National Gallery in London. He also interpreted another grisaille, *The Resurrection of Christ*.

What can one say of the numerous copies made abroad? They are merely increasingly distant reflections that tell nothing of the style or spirit of their creator, but are nevertheless evidence of the lasting success of his work. One can mention three copies made in Holland of *The Rich Kitchen* and *The Poor Kitchen*; The *Sleeping Peddler Robbed by Monkeys* reappears in France, Italy, and Holland. "The Warships" appear in the illustration of *Theatrum orbis terrarum* by Ortelius. Jean-Théodore de Bry includes copies of the *Proverbs* in his *Emblemata secularia* in 1610, and Sadeler introduces a copy of the large landscape *Prospectus Tiburtinus* in two selections of Roman views published in 1606 and 1660.

One should also mention the parodies of Bruegel's work in which monkeys replace men. *The Monkey Alchemist* by Corneille van Thienen is based on a famous plate by Bruegel.

It is often emphasized that Bruegel was in direct line of descent from Hieronymus Bosch, and prints are cited that are transpositions if not of compositions, at least of themes and elements illustrated by the master of Bois-le-Duc.

Jerome Cock published several plates by one or other of the two artists which it is interesting to compare.

The Temptation of St. Anthony (1556) does not bear the name of its "inventor," which has led some critics to put forward Bosch as the author of the original drawing. However, the discovery at the Ashmolean Museum in Oxford of this drawing with Bruegel's signature has destroyed this hypothesis. Cock was to publish in 1561 the engraving of Bosch's composition. The two works are accompanied by the same interpretative verse from Psalm 33; they are, moreover, close in mood and in the adoption of fantastic figures, but Bruegel's personality is clear in the river landscape and the village on either side of the monstrous central theme.

Similar elements are to be found in *Patience*, published in 1557 by Cock, who this time, however, makes specific mention of Bruegel as the artist, Van der Heyden as the engraver, and Cock himself as the publisher. Bruegel adopts the nightmare landscape of Bosch with its whirlwind of deformed creatures and captives, but he situates it in a large landscape composed in his own style. The allegorical figure is portrayed, quite small in size, in the foreground, chained to a block of stone. A maxim taken from Lactantius is inscribed under the picture.

In the same year as his marriage, 1563, Bruegel signed *The Rich Kitchen* and *The Poor Kitchen*, in which he reveals less dependence on Bosch. But he adopts the motif of the round table surrounded by poor creatures incapable of controlling their appetite and stretching out their arms toward the plate loaded with food, a motif which appeared in Cock's 1557 edition of Bosch's *The Large Fishes Devouring the Small Fishes*. It is in a kitchen that Bruegel situates these famished characters obsessed with hunger, while two women are in the process of throwing out a fat bourgeois who would be more in place in *The Rich Kitchen*. In *The Rich Kitchen* Bruegel achieves more powerful expression than Bosch in his *Mardi Gras*, which was to appear in 1567. Several stout individuals are gratifying their senses by giving themselves up to gluttony and breathing in the air that is heavy with the smell of the fat hams attached to the beams and the steam rising from the cooking-pot hanging under the mantlepiece of the vast fireplace. Here it is an unfortunate starveling bagpiper who is being expelled.

The Parable of the Wise and the Foolish Virgins is presented in the form of a diptych. Five busy women spin by lamplight, while on the other side of a central axis the other five dance, having abandoned all work. In response to the call of the three angels, the latter five are halted in front of a dark wall, while the former five are welcomed by a radiant Christ. Heaven is evoked by an architectural composition reminiscent of the constructions that decorate Gothic altarpieces. Bosch had used the same motif in the left leaf of *The Last Judgment* published by Cock.

Finally *The Wedding of Mopsus and Nisa*, a print published after the death of its creator in 1570, recalls the *Two Blind Men* that Cock had engraved from a drawing by Bosch. But Bruegel accentuates the heaviness of the dance steps, the ragged appearance of the participants, and the richness of the natural scene.

The main source of Bruegel's inspiration was the observation of the world about him, in which he lived so intensely. For did he not inscribe on several of his compositions, "*naer 't leven*" ("from life"), to make clear his independence from any academic rules and to show his attachment to the realistic portrayal of both man and nature? He evokes true-to-life peasants, a small world that reveals their life as it is lived in public squares, on their farms, in the fields, and on the roads leading to the villages and suburbs.

Bruegel, the Droll Master, as Van Mander and so many other authors called him, looks on amused and lets us participate in the recreation of mankind.

Jean Galle is careful to mention beneath the second version of the *Skating Scene before the St. George Gate at Antwerp*, "*P. Bruegel delineavit et pinxit ad vivum* 1553." Some doubt has been expressed about this date, which appeared late, at the beginning of the seventeenth century; judging by the style, the drawing is more likely to have been executed about 1559. Tolnay has discovered a drawing dated 1558, but his theories have not been universally accepted by scholars. Whatever the case it is a particularly lively work. The artist portrays a crowd of people skating in all directions, muffled in warm winter cloaks, on the frozen ditches outside one of the gates of the city. Should one see in it a symbolic meaning of mankind skating in all directions—some wisely, some foolishly? For the second version of this print has a motto inscribed in the sky, "The Slipperiness of Human Life."

The dated preparatory drawings and the style enable one to group four plates illustrating man in his amusements around 1559.

The Fair at Hoboken shows a village near Antwerp giving itself up to the celebration of a local fair. A procession is entering the church, a typical example of rural Brabantine Gothic architecture with its heavy bell-tower pierced by a deep portal, raised transept, and gabled chapels. In the square lined with picturesque houses, the festivities are in full swing: men and women are dancing in a ring to the sound of bagpipes, a showman is performing before a gaping crowd, bowmen are engaged in archery, children are eating and rushing about, couples are exchanging confidences. The inn is welcoming visitors; a great banner hangs from its façade bearing the arms of the Hoboken Guild. On a barrel to the left one can make out a monogram "F.H.B.," which is difficult to interpret. Is it the trademark of a brewer, or more likely, the monogram of the engraver Frans Hogenberg, who may have used the drawing by Bruegel as his inspiration? In *The Fair of St. George's Day* the artist adopts the same motifs, but he portrays more episodes and more bustling activity. A double row of booths attracts the gaze of the curious, fencers cross swords, an archery contest is taking place near a windmill, to the right of which appears the outline of a town on the horizon. While some concentrate on the ball game and the hazards of the swings, a large crowd is drinking and dancing at the inn, the façade of which is decorated with the standard of St. George, on which is inscribed the wise exhortation, "Let the Peasants Get Acquainted." The work is filled with episodes spread all over the village square and yet is harmoniously unified in the varied manifestations of the same expression of life and joy.

The Festival of the Fools is inspired by a gathering regularly held in the sixteenth century by the Schools of Rhetoric, the "land juwelen." We are present at an assembly of men outside some covered halls and some houses. To the sound of a small band on a dais, fools are dancing, talking, quarreling, performing their acts. Wherever one looks one sees countless fools. In the foreground a fool with his bauble is taunting another carrying an owl on his wrist.

The festivities of *The Wedding Dance* are also quite wild, but here it is villagers enjoying themselves around a rich bride. Couples are dancing, embracing, servants appear in the background carrying cradles, chairs, and household utensils. It is a slice of country life, a rather gauche but sincere participation in an important family event. *The Masquerade of Ourson and Valentin* recalls a burlesque custom that takes place on the day of the Lent Festival when a girl finally chooses her suitor.

In Brussels Bruegel continued to enjoy popular festivals. Thanks to his drawings, later engraved in 1643 by Hondius, we can experience the unusual and picturesque episode of "The Pilgrimage of the Epileptics to the Church of St. John at Molenbeek." On St. John's Day a procession is organized to the sound of bagpipes to lead the epileptics toward the suburb of Molenbeek. Carnival clowns grimace and dance, fools wield their baubles accompanied by musicians. The stricken follow. If they manage to cross a certain bridge, they will be spared for a year from the affliction of St. John. But the moment they approach what becomes for them an impassable obstacle the pilgrims are seized by fits that convulse their bodies and wring cries from them. Some strong men are taking a firm hold on them in order to help them to cross the bridge. It is an exhausting struggle that demands occasional periods of rest, during which generous people bring refreshments to the epileptics. In these eminently revealing scenes of life, we can sense the amused observation of Bruegel applying himself to portraying the tricks of the fools, the attitudes and strange expressions of the pilgrims, and their helpers.

Bruegel also discovered nature and gave it an original interpretation.

Before Bruegel nature was treated quite conventionally. It provided different planes serving as a frame and above all as a background to religious subjects. In Gérard David, and even more in Quentin Matsys, one sees the beginning of an emancipation. The landscape becomes more important, and the artist expresses a certain emotion in the portrayal of plains, woods, and mountains. Joachim de Patinir gives scarcely any attention to his figures or his subject and establishes landscape as an independent genre. He portrays large panoramic views bristling with masses of rock, but composed of fewer elements than the crowded, imaginative landscapes of Herri met de Bles. Bruegel, faithful to his ideal of communion with living reality, created the realistic landscape in which man is often only a minor element, but in which one can detect the artist's feelings in the presence of the grandeur, the serenity, and the prodigious variety of nature.

In Rome in 1553, Bruegel set to work on two works that were no doubt to be etched and retouched with the burin by their publisher, Georges Hoefnagels. These were *The Rape of Psyche by Mercury* and *The Fall of Icarus*, subjects that are explained by texts taken from Ovid. And yet these subjects are only incidental. Engraved with the burin, the story-telling figures seem to have been added by a less expert hand, not quite achieving unity with the landscape that serves as a framework, however unrelated it may be, to the scenes which justify the titles. A wide river fills the foreground, stretching away in attractive curves that cut into the banks. The surface of the water is enlivened by a number of precisely drawn sailing boats, a barge pulled by three horses, and a raft. The plain extends on both sides in gentle undulations that carry the eye to the distant line of the horizon. Mountainous outcrops crowned with fortified castles proudly dominate the countryside; the villages are concealed in the shade of clumps of trees. Although it takes up only a third of the height of the picture, the sky is enlivened by the decorative movement of the clouds. It is against these clouds that the mythological theme is outlined on a minute scale. Van Bastelaer thought he recognized memories of the Tiber flowing through the Roman countryside in these landscapes, but this opinion is surely influenced by the date and the locality mentioned in the inscription.

There is no doubt, however, that southern sites are recalled in the "Twelve Large Landscapes," to which one can add *The Large Alpine Landscape*, a slightly larger plate than those in the set. These are the first plates illustrating the collaboration of Bruegel and Jerome Cock, who can be considered not only as the publisher but also as the engraver of this set. It is surely to Cock that one must attribute the occasional unsuccessfully portrayed figures that are so poorly integrated with the composition. He must be responsible for the replacing of the vigorous and expressive lines of the original drawings by a more easily executed play of short hatchings to obtain a more facile effect of relief. One must also surely attribute to him the addition of an explanatory title to the story that is introduced almost as an additional episode in the vast landscape.

These plates are striking proof of Bruegel's originality. The iconographic theme is really quite incidental to him; St. Jerome and Magdalen are almost forgotten in the right-hand lower corner, one kneeling on the edge of a wood, the other lying inside a hut made of trunks of fir trees. The Holy Family is resting during the flight into Egypt, as are the three men-at-arms, and seem a little lost in the middle foreground of a brilliant landscape. The pilgrims traveling to Emmaus are seen from behind, again on the edge of a wood. In contrast, nature is the sole object of profound observation by the artist. In the course of his wanderings through the Brabantine countryside, his ride over the Alps, and his stay in various parts of Italy, Bruegel's marveling, sensitive eye led him to make sketches and to take precise note of what he saw. The traveler from the Low Countries must have been overwhelmed by the grandeur of the nature that he came to cross. He understood the sometimes crushing, but always invigorating power of the landscapes that he surveyed in crossing the passes, in following the valleys squeezed between the jagged, tortured mountains, in emerging into widening valleys and onto the plains of Lombardy with their distant horizons. These were the sights that he portrayed, integrating precise recollections into landscapes of his own creation. For very often he includes in them country places, cottages, trees, and inhabitants of his own country. In all this Bruegel reveals, like some of the humanists of his time, an all-embracing curiosity; he is an interpreter of nature in all its variations and riches, a philosopher who contrasts the actions and the petty preoccupations of men with the serenity and power of nature.

Of course, vivid memories of his journey through the mountains impregnate some of the plates in this set more than others. There is a cliff road in *St. Jerome in the Desert*. The view is blocked by a rocky chain falling away steeply to the valley in *The Penitent Magdalen*. *The Alpine Landscape* is constructed in the same way as *The Large Alpine Landscape*. A deep valley snakes through jagged formations of wooded or rocky mountains, leading up to and meeting the sky, which is as tortured as the earth itself. Men, flocks, villages, and trees grouped in clumps or in lines animate with their active presence these impressive, grandiose, and complex landscapes, seen from high above by an eye used to simultaneous observation and composition. The landscape in *The Fowler and His Dog* is very similar. The view of *Tivoli* is a precise recollection of a place that Bruegel loved and brought to life in his own way. For the plate has movement and sound. The noise of the waterfall, the perpetual boiling of the water crashing down onto the rocks, the trees, all are part of the fundamental dynamism of the elements of nature. Only the buildings of the town overlooking them show perfect stability. Recollections of Alpine landscapes are used in other landscapes in this set, but they play a more minor role of wings or backdrop, and memories of Brabant are given increasing and sometimes dominating emphasis. *The Landscape with*

Hare Shooting is treated in the same way. Otherwise he portrays fertile plains, sunken roads, villages with farms with thatched roofs around a Gothic church with its bold bell-tower, stocky peasants driving their heavily laden carts. In *The Wooded Village* all trace of influence of his Italian journey has disappeared. This plate constitutes a real transition heralding the set "Small Landscapes of Brabant and Campine."

These are a good forty realistic representations of rural landscapes of old Brabant, whose considerable success, proved by the numerous editions and interpretations, we mentioned earlier. Beneath vast skies, the calm of which is scarcely disturbed by the flight of a bird, we find the countryside as it was in the sixteenth century: villages hidden away, farms and outbuildings, cottages and castles, inns and windmills lost among the trees, on the edges of fields or of bad roads full of muddy holes. People are portrayed returning from work, sowing, watching their flocks, chopping wood, resting, or shooting with a bow. These true-to-life plates illustrate the calm life of the country and the serenity it inspires. Bruegel is here a historian reporting with precision on a social class working in the normal surroundings of its daily life. Bruegel's drawing is restrained though descriptive, and some of the plates are bathed in a soft light that enlivens the foliage of the willows, maples, and walnut trees.

One comes into more direct contact with the peasants in *Spring* and *Summer*. If some of them are giving themselves up to the pleasures of a country festival, the gardeners are busy with the flowerbeds, preparing for sowing, pruning trees, while the sheep are being shorn. In summer, beneath a blazing sun, the peasants are harvesting and bringing wheat to the village clustered around a charming church with a sturdy tower. In these brilliant plates the human figure assumes its full importance to imbue the landscapes with dynamic life.

The all-embracing curiosity characteristic of Bruegel led him to treat marine scenes, although the sea attracted very few artists of the Flemish School until the nineteenth century.

The *Naval Battle in the Straits of Messina*, the greatest print of the period, is evidence of Bruegel's visit to Sicily, for he evokes the place with quite documentary precision. It also proves his mastery of a broad presentation and layout of a scene. It is hardly necessary to underline again the unity of composition obtained not only by the positioning of the vessels whose wakes match the widening line of the roads and the straits, but also by the play of light and shade on the clouds, the mountains, the waves, and the sails. Although engraved in 1561, the print was executed from a drawing done by Bruegel in 1553.

It is pointless to dwell on the documentary importance of the set of "Warships." The subject had already been exciting interest for a long time. Sets on this theme are known to have been engraved by a Flemish master, a contemporary of Charles the Bold, by Florentine and Venetian artists living at the end of the Quattrocento. But Bruegel, whether he was inspired by the Italian models or not, does more than merely portray the warships with the thousand and one details relative to their construction and armament. These ships, tossed on the waves, which suggest the irresistible power of the ever-moving sea, are silhouetted against vast skies tortured by often menacing clouds or prey to the caprices of the winds. They too become living beings, most decoratively and successfully portrayed. Not surprisingly, "The Fall of Icarus," "Arion on a Dolphin," and "The Fall of Phaëton," episodes added to three of the plates in the set, excite only moderate interest, the incidents hardly emerging from the backgrounds.

If man plays a minor and often incidental role in the landscapes by Bruegel, he becomes in contrast the central object of his observation and thought in the works in which the artist brings his contemporaries to life in discovering the behavior and motives of human beings and understanding their inner life.

The theme of madness was particularly often treated in the sixteenth century by thinkers and writers as well as artists. Bruegel more than once evokes sarcastically the excesses that afflict man. He portrays the interior of a disorderly infirmary where the Dean of Renaix presides over operations for *The Extraction of the Stone of Madness*. Several patients are tied in their chairs, their eyes vacant and faces twisted in pain. The dean and his assistants are carrying out the extraction of this accursed tumor; an owl, symbolic of the darkness in which the minds of these poor beings are plunged, is seen in the center of the composition, which is of mediocre technical quality. The plate entitled *The Witch of Malleghem* is far superior, revealing a remarkable sureness of line, as well as an uncommonly powerful imagination. The crowd of men is pressing forward, carried away by their passions and madness, to undergo the treatment of an astute shrew who is reputed to cure anxiety. As a contrast in the background there appear a church and some houses in a peaceful wood. *The Alchemist*, consulting his tomes, is frantically trying with his assistants to transmute gold with the help of the Philosopher's Stone; he is forgetting his duty toward his penniless family that has to be taken into the "lospital" (poorhouse), for the alchemist, an eternal utopian, has failed in everything, as is confirmed by an inscription in one of the books resting on his desk to the right, "al ghemist." Bruegel here allows himself a play on words admirably illustrated in one of his most brilliant compositions. Monsters, witches, madmen, lewd animals, inhabitants of the underworld populate the mysterious den of the magician Hermogenes, who is abandoning himself to his mad experiments. St. Jacob, the pilgrim, resists this stupefying vision as does St. Anthony his temptations. He is about to intervene to re-establish order. In an extraordinary rumpus and in the middle of an infernal dance, we watch *The Fall of the Magician Hermogenes*. It can be presumed that in these two works Bruegel has borrowed many a picturesque detail from the mystery plays of his time.

It is not only madness that afflicts man, but also sloth, gluttony, drunkenness, and egoism. Bruegel, who observed from life the sad or humorous consequences of these passions and noted the attitudes of those who succumbed to them, portrays them and describes in an often amusing, but also very accurate, way the nature and effect of their behavior. In order to be more easily understood his compositions often illustrate well-known proverbs that are often repeated without attention to the wisdom they contain.

A schoolmaster is surrounded by a miniature world whose appearance and clothing call to mind burghers or monks rather than children. They are trying to spell and read, but many of them prefer to argue, play tricks on each other, or even do nothing at all. The master intervenes only to punish a pupil. All this takes place before an ass, which, without its spectacles and by the light of a candle, is attempting to decipher some notes of music, for the plate portrays *The Ass at School*. The ass can be the attribute of sloth, but also the symbol of ignorance and incompetence. A fifteenth-century dictum says, "An ass understands nothing in music." *The Sleeping Peddler Is Robbed by Monkeys*, for "while the peddler takes his rest, the monkeys cast his goods to the wind." This theme was represented among the "side-dishes" at the marriage of Charles the Bold and Margaret of York in 1468, and it had also been used by engravers. In his turn Bruegel evokes "the story of the dreamer who loses his goods as he sleeps." The traveling peddler has lazily fallen asleep before entering the village; the monkeys take advantage of this to appropriate the most varied objects that they are removing from his provision basket.

The frequenters of *The Rich Kitchen*, or those being chased out of *The Poor Kitchen*, are not the only gluttons. There are also those who live in *Luilekkerland, or the Land of Plenty*. The intellectual has laid down his books and formulae, the peasant has stretched out on his flail, the man-at-arms has abandoned his lance. They are digesting their food and taking their ease. A whole chicken is disappearing, ready cooked, into the mouth of the personage with the raised visor who is sheltering beneath a roof covered with pies. The sea is milk, the mountain on the left an enormous bread pudding, the hedge is made of sausage, the fat plants are cakes. A well-fattened pig is lumbering along, for it is the symbol of gluttony, and Ripa says, "Like this animal which seeks only to satisfy the appetites of its mouth, a man dominated by sloth abandons himself completely to the gratification of the senses, thereby assuring the loss of his good name."

This meditation on human life continues. Everyman, *Elck*, looks after himself, his own interests, retreats into a barrel to investigate its riches more thoroughly, pulls the blanket over to his side; he pays no attention to his fellows, and worse still none to himself. This carefully engraved plate was executed from two vigorous drawings, signed by Bruegel in 1558, of well-balanced composition and rich in delicate observation. The weak are exposed to the crushing brutality of the strong. *The Large Fishes Devouring the Small Fishes* is recalled by Bruegel in a famous plate inspired by Hieronymus Bosch. The principal subject fills the whole width of the foreground. In a boat an old man is pointing out the scene to a young child, his gesture explained by an "Ecce" ("Look here") inscribed beneath the big fish, whose mouth and side are pouring forth smaller fish that have in their turn swallowed even smaller ones. Light and shade play on the scales of the large fish, whose backbone forms a loosely drawn arc. In the background a port is outlined against the horizon. If all is simple and at rest in this work, by contrast *The Battle of the Moneybags and Strongboxes* is a scene of confusion and fighting; men-at-arms, strongboxes, and moneybags brutally and avidly tear each other open.

It has been remarked that from 1556 Bruegel becomes increasingly interested in human life. He undertakes sets constituting real encyclopedias, cycles of life.

The set of "Flemish Proverbs" in the Berlin Museum dates from 1559. It was in 1568 that Jean Wierix published seven circular engravings, with another five no doubt added by Pierre van der Heyden, forming the set of "Twelve Flemish Proverbs." In each composition one or two characters appear in an interior or more often in the foreground of a town or country scene. With a few incisive lines, expressive poses, and explanatory gestures, the proverbs are illustrated and are easily understood, transformed into living reality, set in a familiar frame, and enacted by men universal to all time. Sentences in Dutch explain all the proverbs; French texts accompany the first seven plates. "A quarrelsome woman brings only trouble to the house." "There is always a way to a rich man's money." "I wear mourning at the sight of the dishonesty of men." "The music of a rich man is always pleasant even when he plays on a jawbone." "A: Look at my excellent nets and floats, just what you need. B: Go and sell somewhere else, and take your merchandise with you." "One begs in vain at the door of the deaf." "He who often gives without return, wastes another arrow to retrieve the first." With no other guide the two blind men fall into a ditch full of water; a drunken fool is hatching a large egg that contains only a bauble; the peddler neglecting his customer is like the fiancé who is idly scratching his head beside his love; the hay running after the horse is as contrary as the woman chasing the man; the egoist sits and warms himself while the house burns. One could add to this set the engraving, circular or rectangular in shape, *The Drunken Peasant Locked into a Pigsty* by peasants shouting their disapproval.

Humanity is divided like the "wise virgins and the foolish virgins." Virtue attracts some, vice subjugates others. In his turn Bruegel treats the great theme which, throughout the history of iconography, has attracted so many artists of every period of the Christian era. We are not observing an exercise in psychology; the virtues and vices are not presented as triumphing. Bruegel takes his place among the artists of the Middle Ages; he sets in motion an imposing number of personages whom he subjects in simultaneous scenes to the most varied episodes, illustrating "The Seven Capital Sins" and "The Seven Theological and Cardinal Virtues." In the foreground of each plate a personage, easily identifiable by the attributes it is carrying, symbolizes vice or virtue; in addition the theme is indicated by its Latin name.

Popular sayings and customs inspire several of the episodes as do the mystery plays of the period. The spirit of Hieronymus Bosch, his world of monstrous personages, his infernal visions, have a more direct influence on "The Seven Capital Sins." The real is freely intermixed with the fantastic. The causes and consequences of *Wrath, Sloth, Pride, Avarice, Gluttony, Envy, Lust* are evoked by varied but always humorous or terrifying images. The bear is an attribute of anger, and the crescent moon appearing on a shield recalls that it is this heavenly body that excites and controls the anger and folly of man; the sword and the torch symbolize all the destruction taking place on earth and even in the sky; only water, to the left, presents a calm surface. The slothful woman rests on a donkey, while snails surround her. The monsters that plague man in his enjoyment often take the form of a fantastic animal. Pride is admiring herself in a mirror, isolated in her arrogance. Counterfeit money is being piled in chests and sacks, greedy men quarrel over the treasure, Avarice no longer bothers to weigh her gold, a large toad crawling forward in the foreground announces death. The woman symbolizing Gluttony is drinking greedily, while a wild boar she is standing on and a dog fight over turnips falling from a wooden tub. By eating and drinking to excess man is preparing his own destruction. Jealousy is gnawing a heart, while pointing at a strutting turkey. Envy is a plague leading to death. The garden of love or delight becomes a terrifying vision, the naked woman is giving herself to a monster with a fish's head. Man's evil instincts lead him to expiations that come from the realm of infernal nightmare.

The original drawings of these plates exist, as do those which Jerome Cock used to publish "The Seven Theological and Cardinal Virtues." Although the name of Pierre van der Heyden appears as the engraver in "The Seven Capital Sins," it is not found in the following set, even though Jerome Cock was the publisher of both sets. Critics are uncertain whether it is the work of Van der Heyden or Philippe Galle. Whatever the case, the monsters inspired by Bosch have disappeared, portrayals of contemporary life predominate, the design of the compositions is more grandiose, and the drawing is clearly superior. Faith wears the habit of a nun, the Tables of Moses rest on her head, she is pointing to the Scriptures on which the Dove has alighted; assembled around her are the instruments of the Passion. Inside a church the crowd throngs around a preacher, while the Sacraments are conferred. Composure and simplicity mark this print that so accurately evokes the reality and profundity of a place of worship in the sixteenth century. Hope stands on an anchor, she is holding agricultural tools, on her head is a beehive. Haven is close for the men buffeted by the stormy seas, deliverance is at hand for the prisoners, the fire will soon be under control, food will be given to those fishing and working. Charity is carrying a flaming heart and is crowned with a pelican, she is welcoming the poor children, while around her in the village square the seven works of mercy are being enacted: the starving are being fed, the thirsty satisfied, the prisoners are being consoled by their relatives, the dead are being buried, the pilgrims welcomed, the sick visited, the naked clothed. Justice on a pedestal carries a sword and is blindfolded. She is presiding over the varied punishments ordered by a court that seems pitiless rather than merciful. All the legal practices of the sixteenth century are re-enacted before our eyes: torture, mutilation, whipping, strappado, beheading, hanging, the rack, and burning at the stake. Prudence wears a sieve on her head, she is admiring herself in a convex mirror, but holds a coffin in her other hand, her feet rest on a ladder. Can one not detect a note of sarcasm in the artist's study of the earthbound preoccupations of men obsessed with materialistic considerations? Fortitude is overcoming a dragon; wings add to his power; the breastplate, pillar, and anvil are customary attributes. An irresistible force drives those who are pursuing men and monsters bent on destruction. Temperance, carrying a clock on her head, is holding reins and a pair of glasses, her foot is resting on the sail of a windmill. She is surrounded by animated groups. Tolnay maintains that they are a derisive representation of the seven liberal arts, while Lebeer insists on the concept of measure that corresponds with temperance, the mean sought by calculators, grammarians, musicians, dialecticians, rhetoricians, geometers, astronomers, those children of the planet Mars.

The plate of *The Last Judgment* was engraved in 1558, that is, in between the two sets just discussed. In it one finds again the tendencies of the set "The Seven Capital Sins." For the foreground is occupied by a man and a woman imploring Heaven, but especially by the monstrous creatures marked forever by the vices to which they abandoned themselves. The procession of the chosen represented in their naked reality is guided by an angel toward the dawn. A rather small St. Michael is busy moving aside the great crowd of those, led by a torch and pikes, who are waiting to take their place in the boat. On each trip the boat unloads into the viscous mouth of a giant fish the terrified humans who are dragged out by fantastic creatures with heads of fishes or toads. The supreme Judge, the angels, and the watchers in Heaven are portrayed in the traditional form passed down from the late Middle Ages.

Bruegel composed several religious themes that were published by Cock, Galle, Perret, and later by Visscher. These few pictures reflect perfectly the mind and style of the master.

The goodness of Christ carrying the lamb on his shoulders as he emerges from the sheepfold is emphasized in *The Parable of the Good Shepherd*. In the background of the scene, on either side of the central building, Bruegel contrasts the terror of the sherpherd abandoning his flock to the attacking wolves with the vigor of the one using his crook to strike the dangerous enemy of his sheep. Around the sheepfold we witness scenes of pillage; like the wolves, men are attacking the decrepit hut, breaking through the clay walls and the thatched roof to steal the sheep. Christ, surrounded by his trusting flock, is portrayed in the gaping opening of the fold. *Jesus and the Adulteress* recalls the famous words, "Let him who is without sin cast the first stone." Scribes and Pharisees are showing very different reactions; the crowd is ignoring this episode, pretending to attend to its business and leaving the scene. The pose of the woman whose elegant dress falls in folds is full of trust and gratitude for the understanding of Christ, who is writing on the ground the sentence that is so comforting to sinful humanity. Christ walks with the *Pilgrims on the Road to Emmaus*. He delivers those suffering infernal tortures in the *Descent into Limbo*. *The Risen Christ* casts back darkness, stupefies the guards at the moment when the angel, seated on the rock that has been rolled back, announces to the holy women that the tomb is empty.

Already among his contemporaries, and certainly from Van Mander onward, Pieter Bruegel was the subject of comment. What sort of man was he? What were his ideas? Does he express in his work any part of his desires and concepts?

Critical analysis of his paintings, drawings, and engravings has led experts on his work to adopt very different positions. It is true that a psychological and historical study of this nature is one of the most difficult to conduct. Let us first consider the problem of his prints, especially as these constitute an important group that moreover reveals a strong unity in the conception of subject as well as in composition and execution. It should be remembered that these drawings, so often dated and signed, were produced by Bruegel with such concern for the final details that the engravers had merely to reproduce rather than interpret his work.

Consideration of his engravings reveals that in all the subjects he portrayed, Bruegel applied his special gift of penetrating observation to understanding nature and man.

Some critics, and among them Van Mander, maintain that it is the picturesque elements of the countryside and the "droll" side of the peasant that captivated the artist. He was the amused, story-telling chronicler of a group of his contemporaries whom he portrayed in the normal surroundings of their life. In this case Bruegel would have to be classed among the "minor masters" and included among the historians of folklore and popular life.

Others feel his work to be full of allusions to the political and social conditions of his period. These interpreters discover comments on the hardships due to the reign of Philip II and the rebellious spirit of a people sworn to opposition.

Others find that Bruegel reveals through a certain hermetism his allegiance to the free-thinking and freedom-seeking societies of Antwerp. He is supposed to have professed his support of an ideal of emancipation from all dogma, believing in man free from all religious attachment whose life is based on moral dignity.

For the last forty years or so critics have insisted on Bruegel's scholarship, wishing to recognize in him the mind of a true philosopher. Some speak freely of his cosmic vision, of his conception of the "underworld" that is revealed in subjects treating the kingdom of fools, which apes and reverses the ways and customs of the kingdom of the wise.

But is not the truth, insofar as one can ascertain it in such an intimate and delicate sphere, more full of nuance and less exclusive?

Bruegel was without doubt of peasant stock, but in studying his work one cannot deny him a certain culture and scholarship. His journey to and in the Italian peninsula demonstrates his interest in all the varied aspects of the Alpine, Roman, Neapolitan, and Sicilian landscapes. His faithful collaboration with Jerome Cock kept him in contact with the most diverse intellectual and artistic circles in Antwerp. Emphasis has been laid on his relations with his friend, who so sincerely mourned his death, Ortelius, the geographer, but one can legitimately quote other names, among them that of the humanist illuminator Giulio Clovio. Bruegel lived among painters impressed by the ideals of the Italian Renaissance and molded by their contact with learned treatises. He was well aware of the moralizing, didactic literature of his time, as well as the theatrical presentations of the rhetoricians, and he sought inspiration from them more than once in his engravings.

But Bruegel did not live by the theories proposed by his contemporaries. He wanted to be independent. In Italy it was nature that impassioned him. Strange to say, one can find no trace of precise memories of the Italian masters in his compositions, for the links proposed by Tolnay with various works of

Michelangelo are not conclusive. The engraving published by Philippe Galle after his death in 1574, *The Triumph of Time or of Saturn*, could not be further from the scholarly conceptions of the Italian Renaissance.

Bruegel is clearly to be classed more in the tradition of the national school, not in its Italianized tendencies, but in the line of Hieronymus Bosch. Thanks to the master of Bois-le-Duc, he penetrated the infernal world, the domain of monstrous shapes born of nightmare, the visions created by an astounding imagination. But he was never so dominated by it as to become a mere continuator.

His greatest source of inspiration, which guaranteed his independence and assured his originality, was life itself, *"naer 't leven, ad vivum"* ("from life"), as he could with justification inscribe on his compositions.

It is the enormous variety of nature that he celebrates in his Alpine, maritime, or Brabantine landscapes. He expresses its strength, its power, luxuriance, chaos, vastness, intimacy, rustic peace. Mountains, seas, rivers, valleys, fields, and woods are endowed with vital energy, with dynamic strength. And this is how Bruegel establishes a relationship between nature and man. How small man can seem before these landscapes! Nature seems unaware of the human drama; she serves as a frame for it and often even offers man a lesson in moderation, in tranquility.

In compositions where man is the central element, Bruegel portrays peasants, simple men who quite naturally and straightforwardly play out the game of life, expressing their desires, passions, and aspirations. Bruegel, the psychologist, silhouettes aspects and attitudes taken from real models attached to their daily life, to their customs, and to their work. He examines the hearts and minds of men involved in everyday actions, and Bruegel, the philosopher, discovers that it is man's lot to sway between good and evil. In the background of the print *Elck* there is seen, on one side, a church in the peace of a wooded village, on the other, an encampment of soldiers preparing to fight and destroy. Bruegel shows his contemporaries struggling to make the decision that will direct and control their lives. These men do not give themselves up to speculation, abstract ideas, or an intellectualism beyond their understanding; they practice the wisdom of common sense and try to live out the lessons offered by the popular proverbs that are the philosophy of the simple. Bruegel represents these people humorously; on occasion he pokes fun at those who are unsuccessfully or falsely trying to do good. This reflective artist uses sarcasm to teach men of all ages to know themselves better.

BIBLIOGRAPHICAL NOTES

There are innumerable works on Pieter Bruegel the Elder. A list of these can be found in the bibliography compiled by H. van HALL, *Repertorium voor de geschiedenis der Nederlandsche schilder- en graveerkunst sedert het begin der 12de eeuw tot het eind van 1946* (The Hague, 1936–49). Among monographs on the painter, draftsman, and engraver, we cite: Rene van BASTELAER and Georges H(ULIN) de LOO, *Peter Bruegel l'Ancien, son oeuvre et son temps (Brussels, 1907)*; R. van BASTELAER, *Les Estampes de Peter Bruegel l'Ancien* (Brussels, 1908); F. W. H. HOLLSTEIN, *Dutch and Flemish Etchings, Engravings, and Woodcuts*, vol. III (Amsterdam, 1951); K. von TOLNAY, *Die Zeichnung Pieter Bruegels* (2nd ed.; Zurich, 1952); P. GROSSMANN, *The Painting of Brueghel* (London, 1955); L. MUENZ, *Bruegel, the Drawings* (London, 1961). Mention must be made of all the articles by L. LEBEER (see the list of these publications in *Le Cabinet des Estampes, Trente années d'acquisitions, 1930–1960*, Brussels, Bibliothèque Royale de Belgique, 1961), which foreshadow a book awaited from this author on the prints of Bruegel; we note in particular L. LEBEER, *Les Estampes de Pierre Bruegel l'Ancien*, in the *Annales de la Société royale d'archéologie de Bruxelles*, XLV, 1941, pp. 154–80. For the method, see Ch. TERLINDEN, *Pierre Bruegel le Vieux et l'histoire*, in the *Revue belge d'archéologie et d'histoire de l'art*, XII, 1942, pp. 229–57. As a general work on the Antwerp school of engraving, we cite A. J. J. DELEN, *Histoire de la gravure dans les anciens Pays-Bas et dans les provinces belges. Le XVIe siècle* (Paris, 1934–35).

PHOTOGRAPHICAL SOURCES

PIETER BRUEGEL THE ELDER

All photographs have been supplied by the Bibliothèque Royale, Brussels, except for the following:
Bibliothèque Nationale, Paris: 136, 137, 159–62
Rijksmuseum, Amsterdam: 34, 48, 113, 130, 151–57.

PLATES

1

2

LVBRICITAS VITÆ HVMANÆ. LA LVBRICITE DE LA VIC HVMAINE. DE SLIBBERACHTIGHEYT VAN S MENSCHEN LEVEN

PORTA S. GEORGII ANTVERPIÆ. 1553.

5

H cork excudi

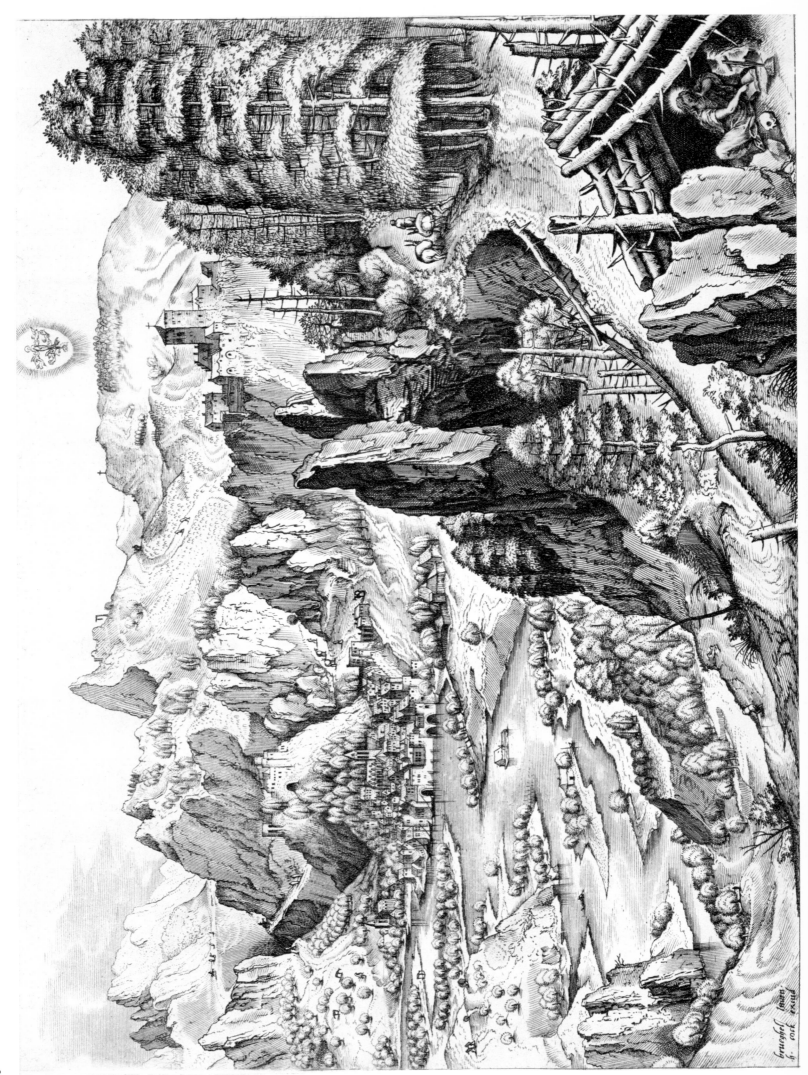

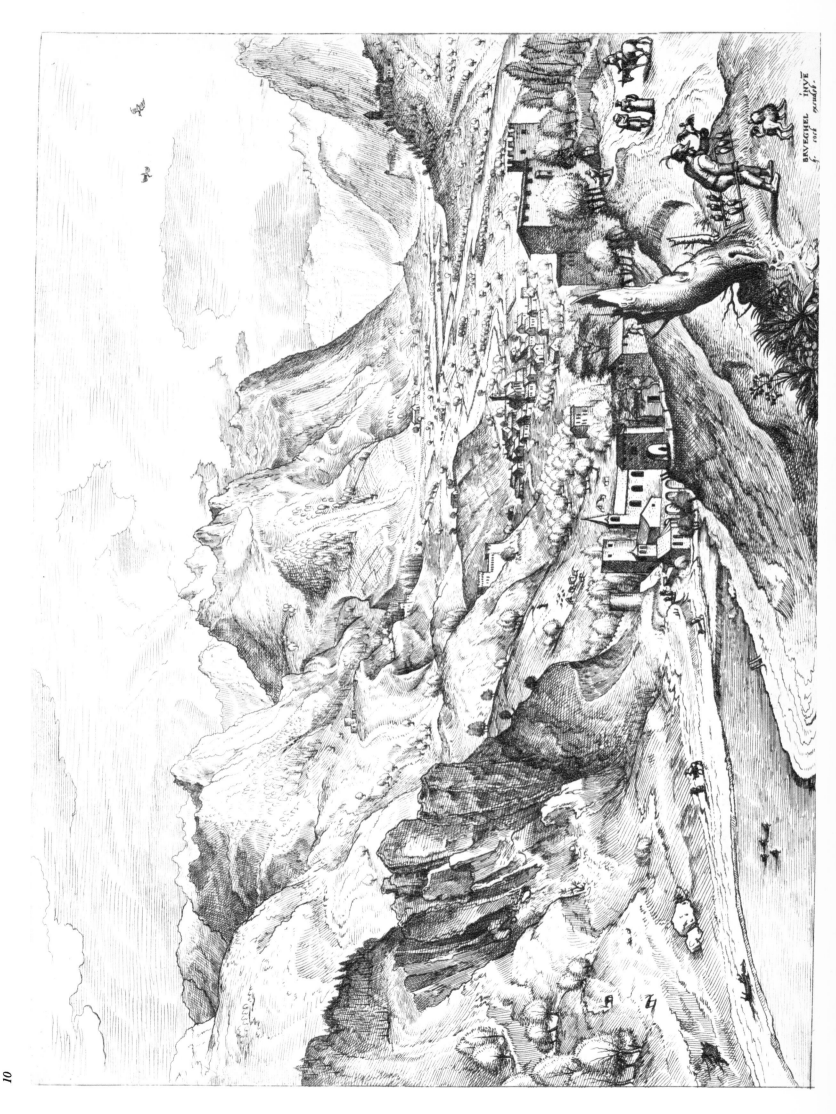

BRVEGHEL INVE
f. ad. Arialt.

BRVEGHEL . INVE
H. cock excud.

11

Brueghel. fecit
M. Cock excu.

12

14

brueghel inue
H. cock excud.

15

18

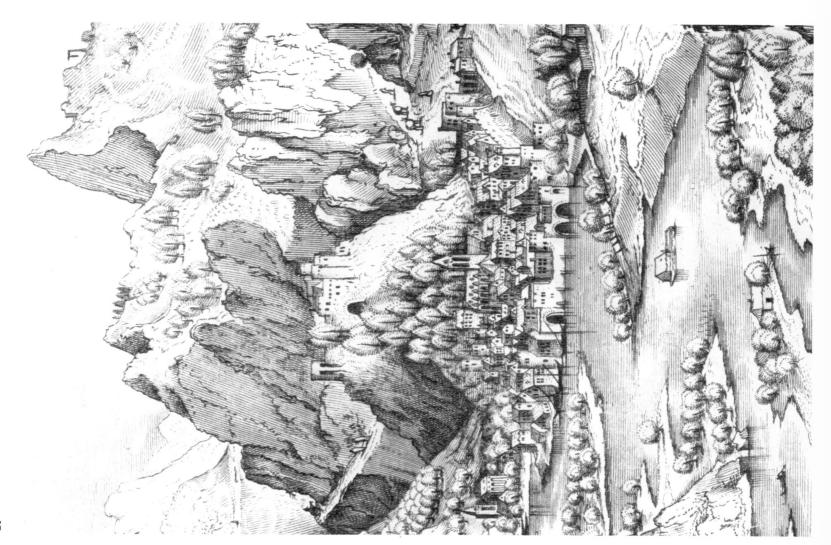

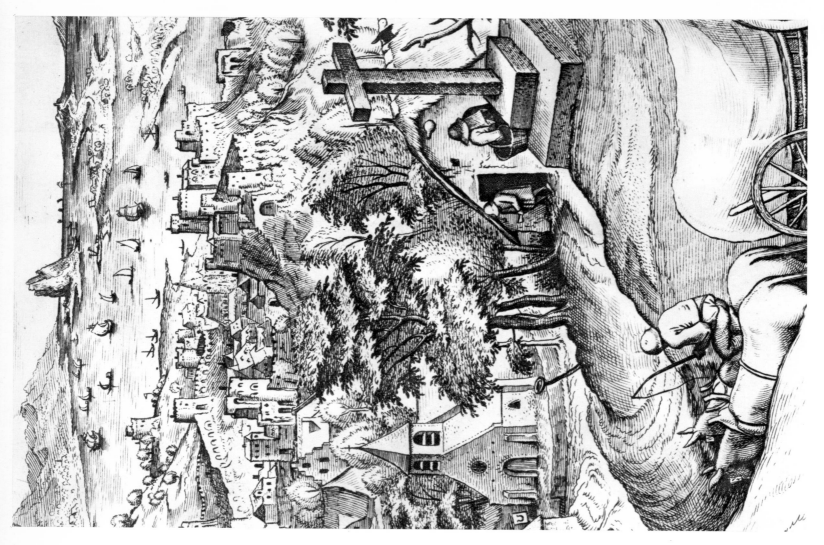

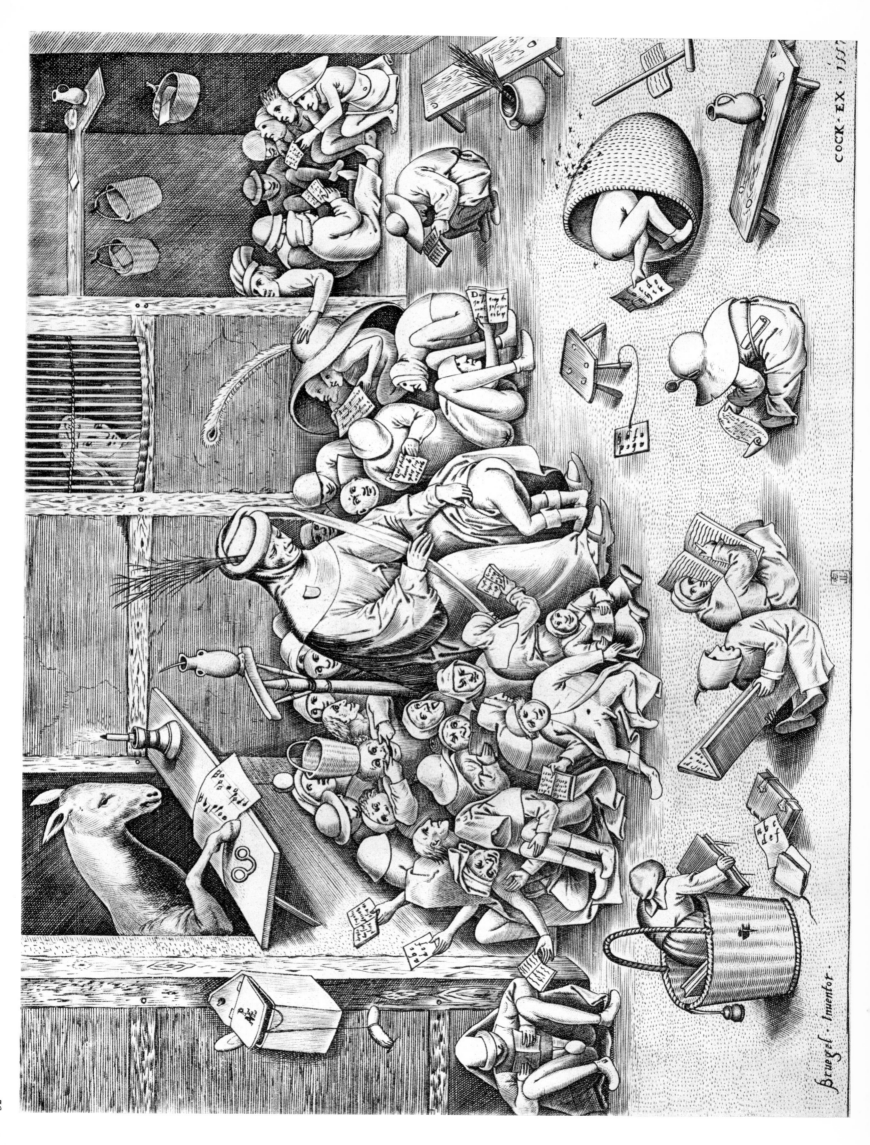

32

Bruegel · Inuentor ·

COCK · EX · 1557

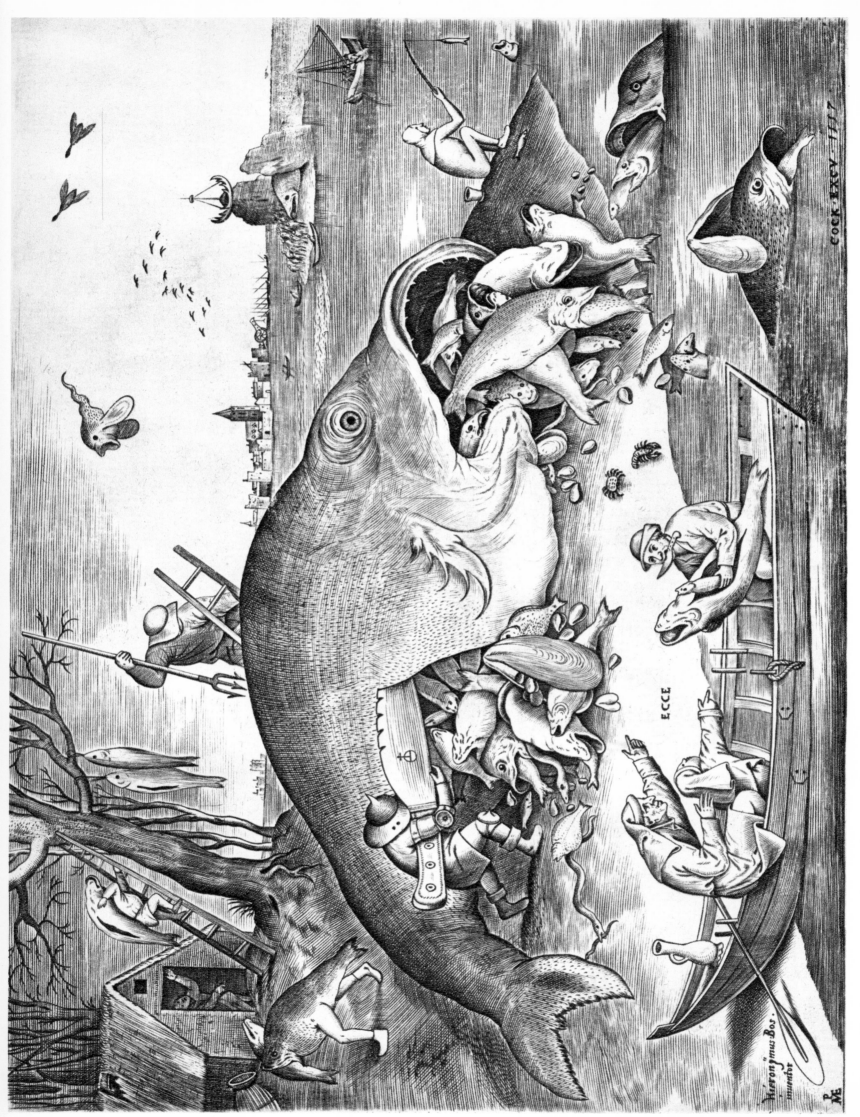

Hieronijmus Bos.
inuentor

ECCE

COCK EXCV 1557

33

34

PATIENTIA

H. Cock. excude. 1557.   Brueghel. Inuent.

35

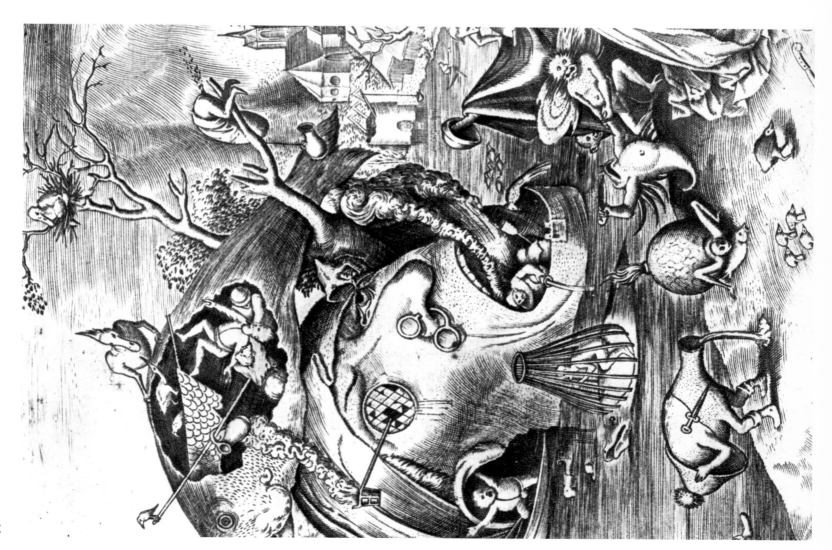

BRVEGEL INVE.

38

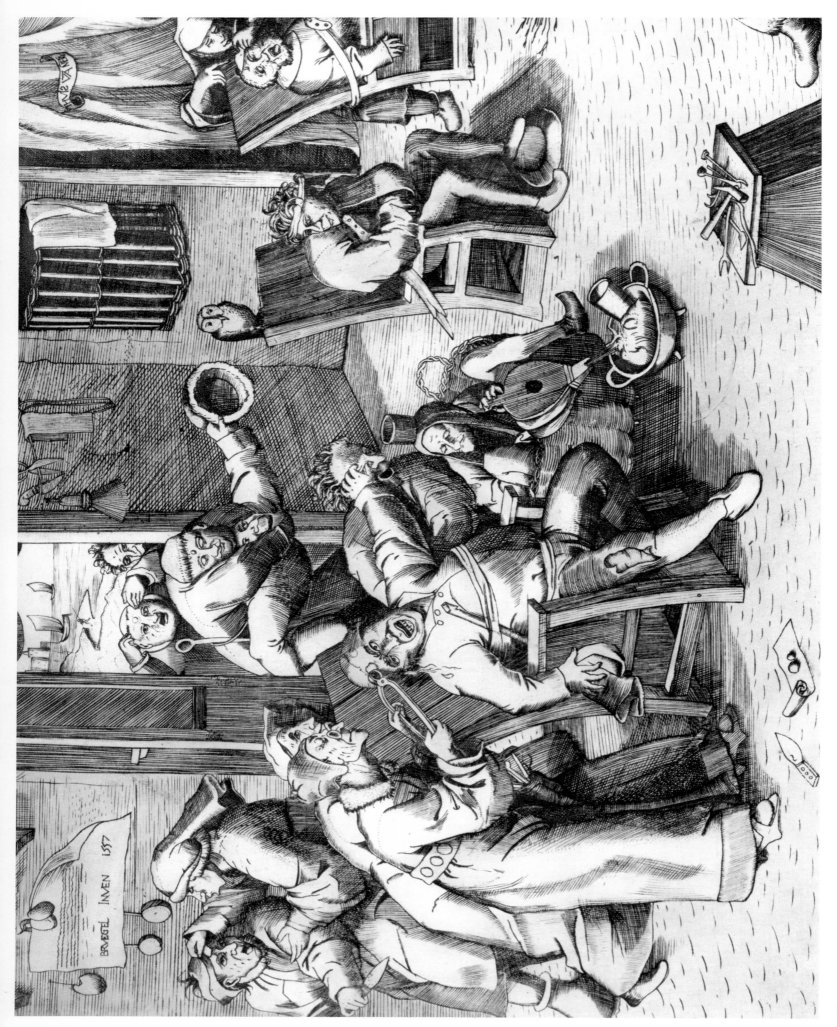

41

P. brueghel. Inuentor.

IRA

H. Cock. excude. Cum. gratia. et. priuilegio. · 1558 ·

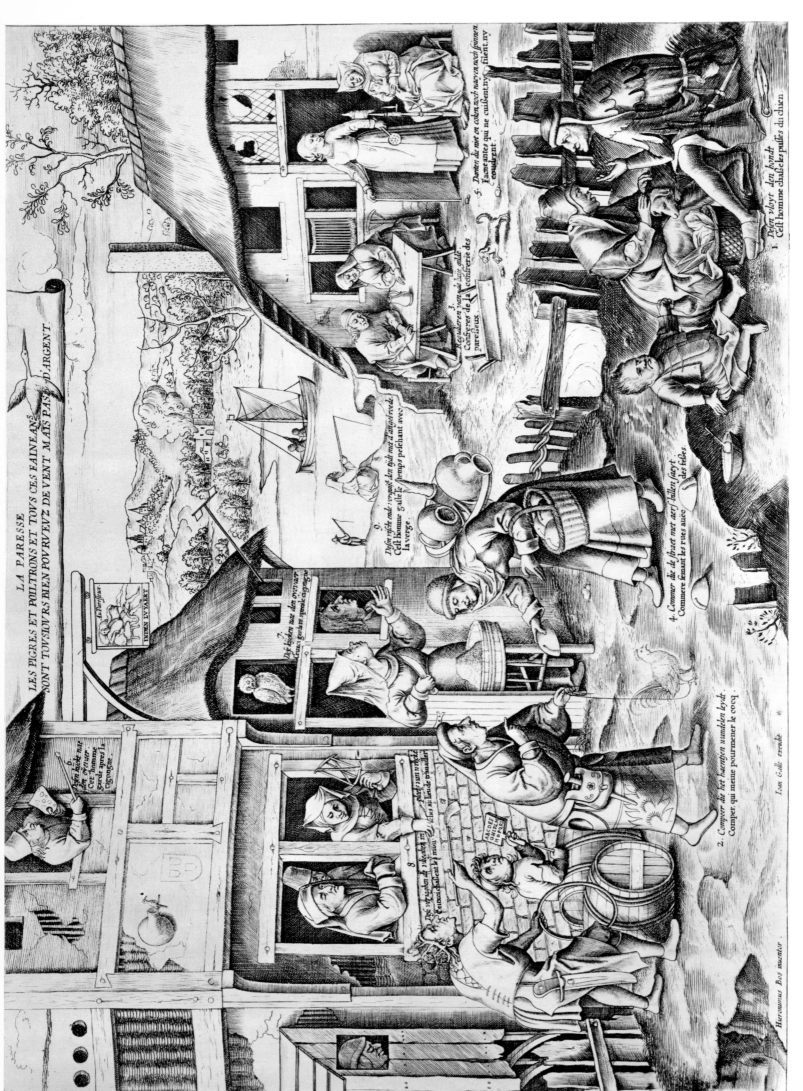

SVPERBIA.

P. brueghel. Inuentor.

Cock excud cum priuilg 1558

AVARITIA

P. brueghel. Inuentor.

Cock. excud. cum priuileg. 1558.

GVLA·

H. Cock. excud. cum gratia et privilegie · 1558

45

INVIDIA.

Brueghel. invent.

Cock. excud. cum priuil.

46

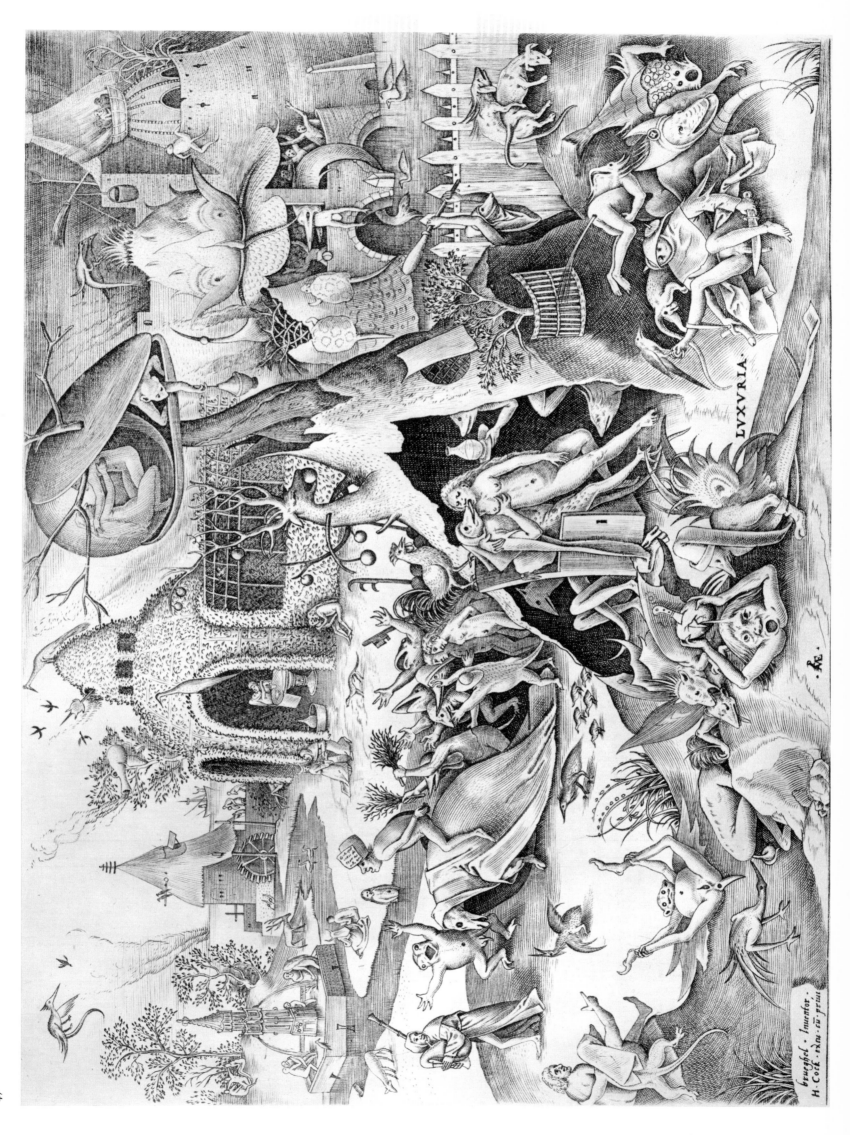

LVXVRIA.

Bruegel. Inuentor.
H. Cock. exu. cū preui[?]

47

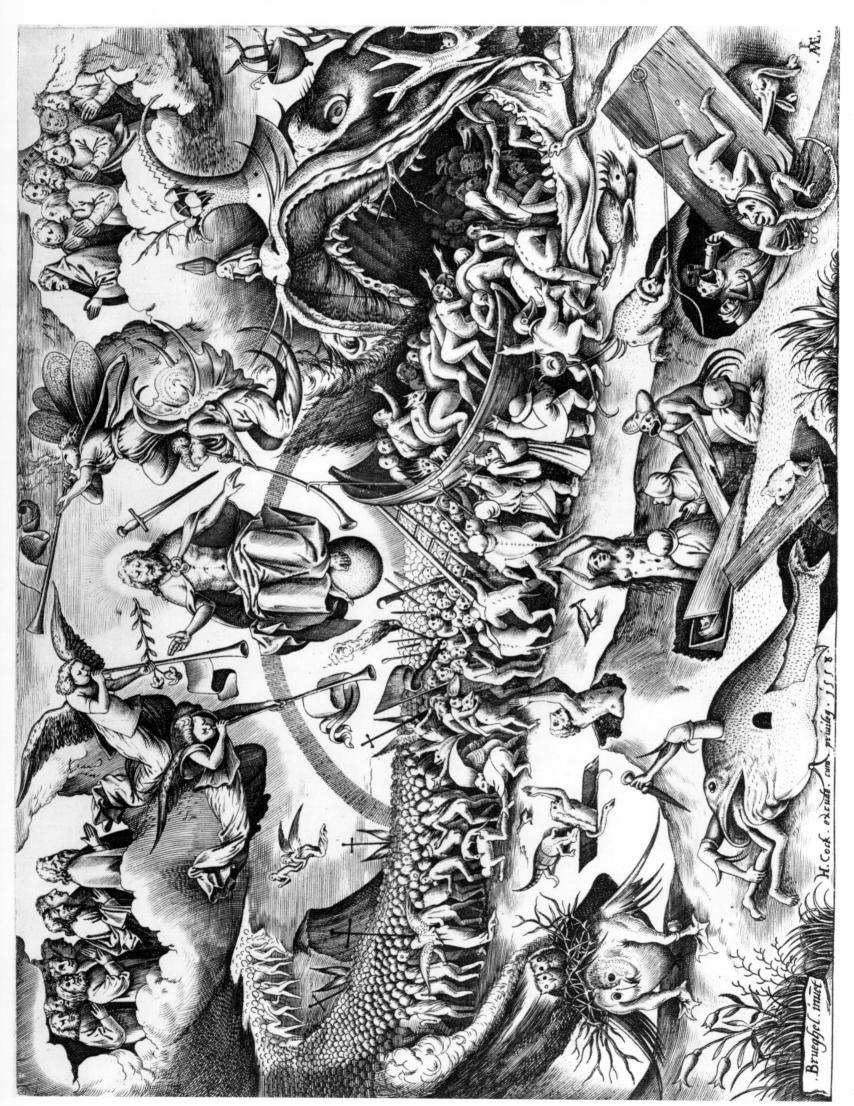

Brueghel inuet   H.Cock. excud . cum priuileg . 1 5 5 8

PRIVATVM COMMODVM.
LE PROVFIT PARTICVLIER.
EYGHEN BAET.

NEMO NON SEIPSVM

NIEMAT·EN·KENT·HE·SELVE

NEMO NON III

QVILIBET CHASCUN ELCK.

P. Bruegel invent.

Ioan. Galle. excudit.

49

50

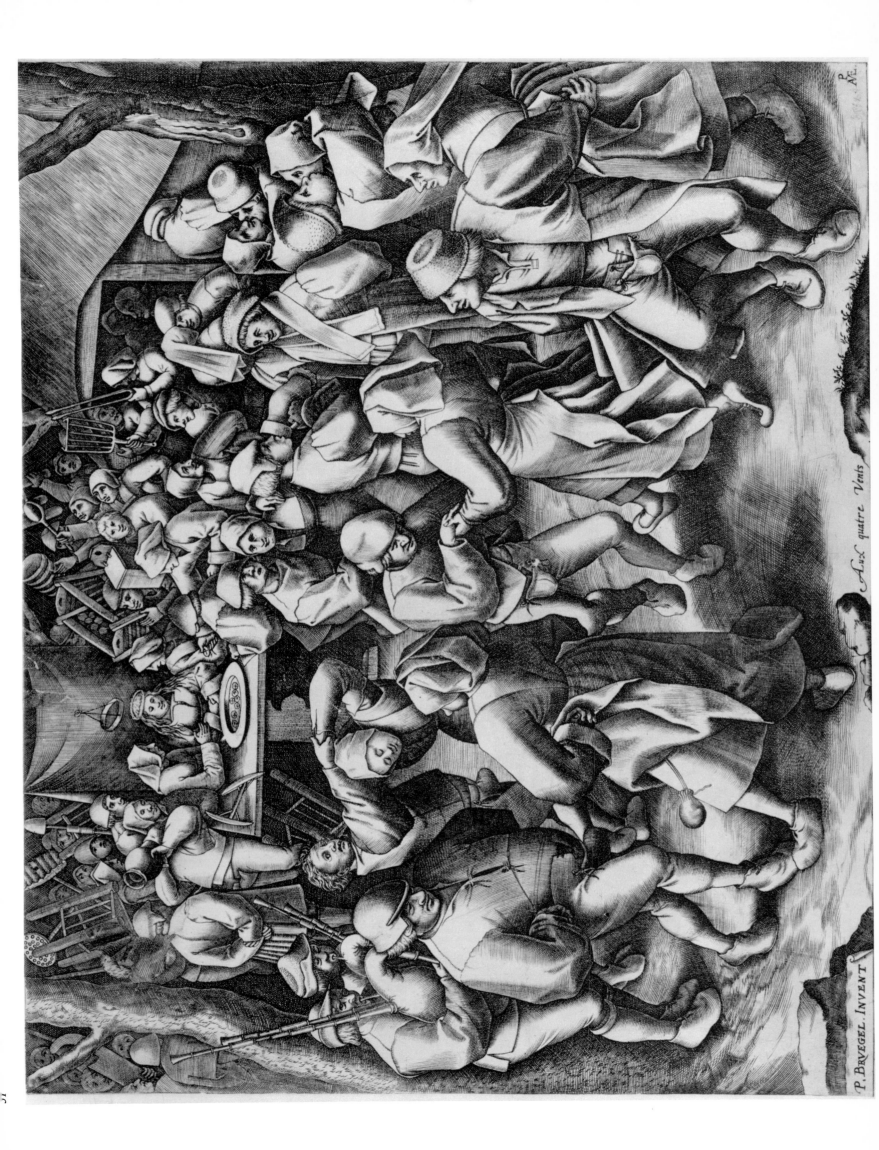

P. BRVEGEL. INVENT   Aux quatre Vents   P. AE.

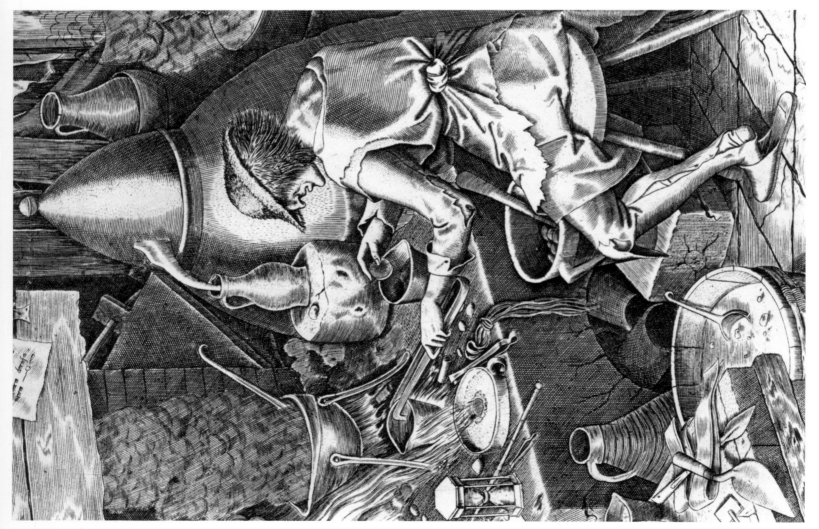

P. Brueghel Inventor   Aux quatre Vents.   .AE.

55

Dit is Guide van

Bruegel

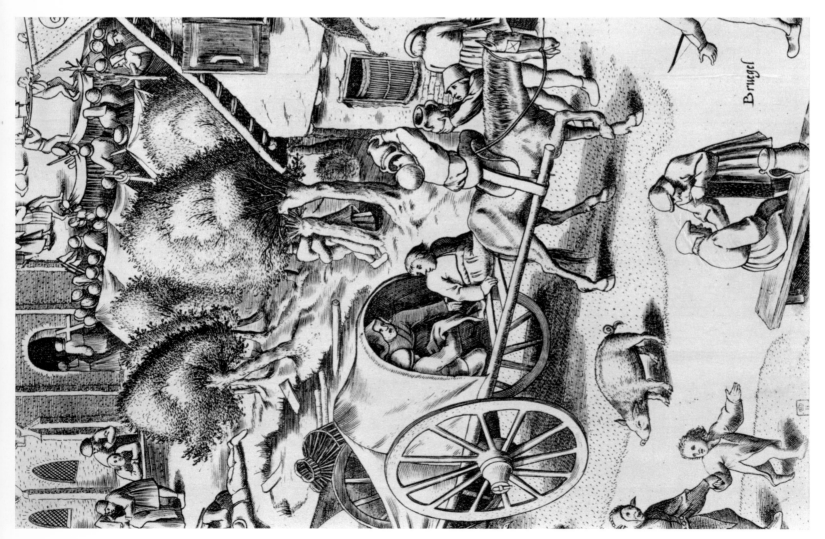

Bruegel

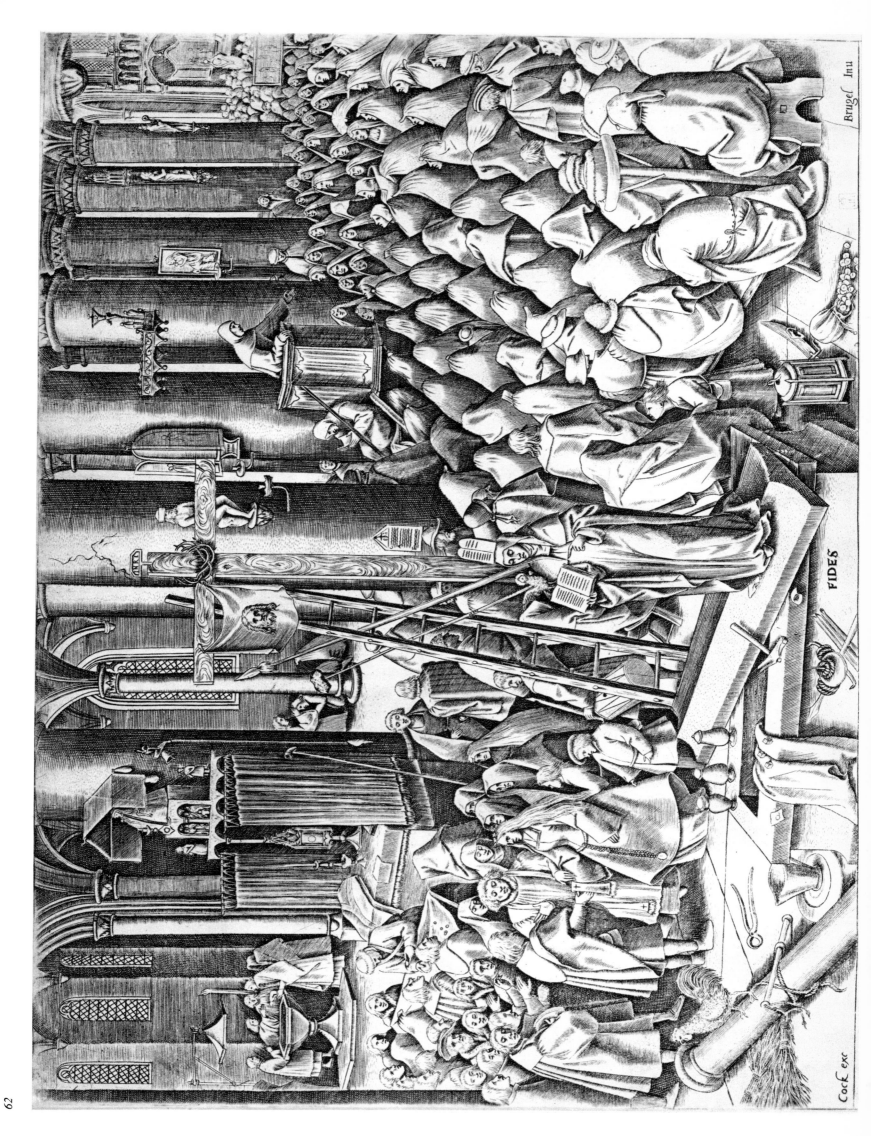

FIDES

Cock exc

Brugel Inu

62

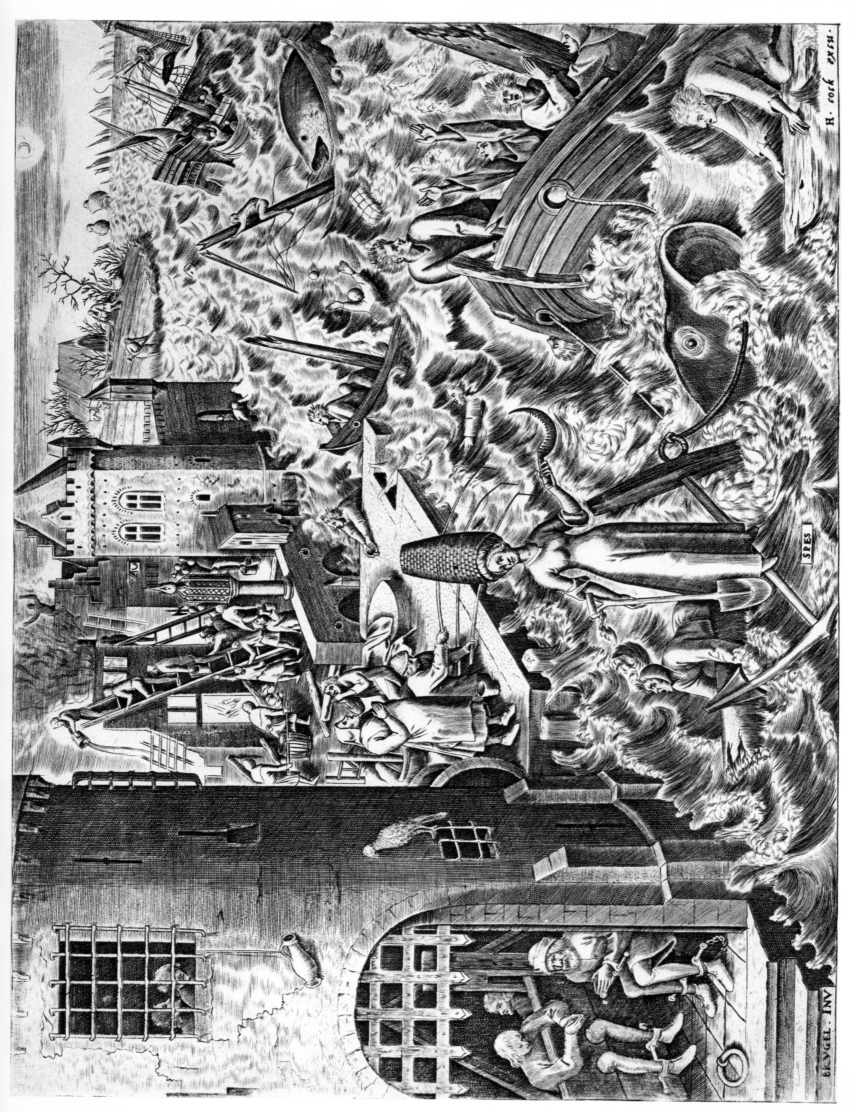

SPES

H. cock excu.

BRVGEL. INV

63

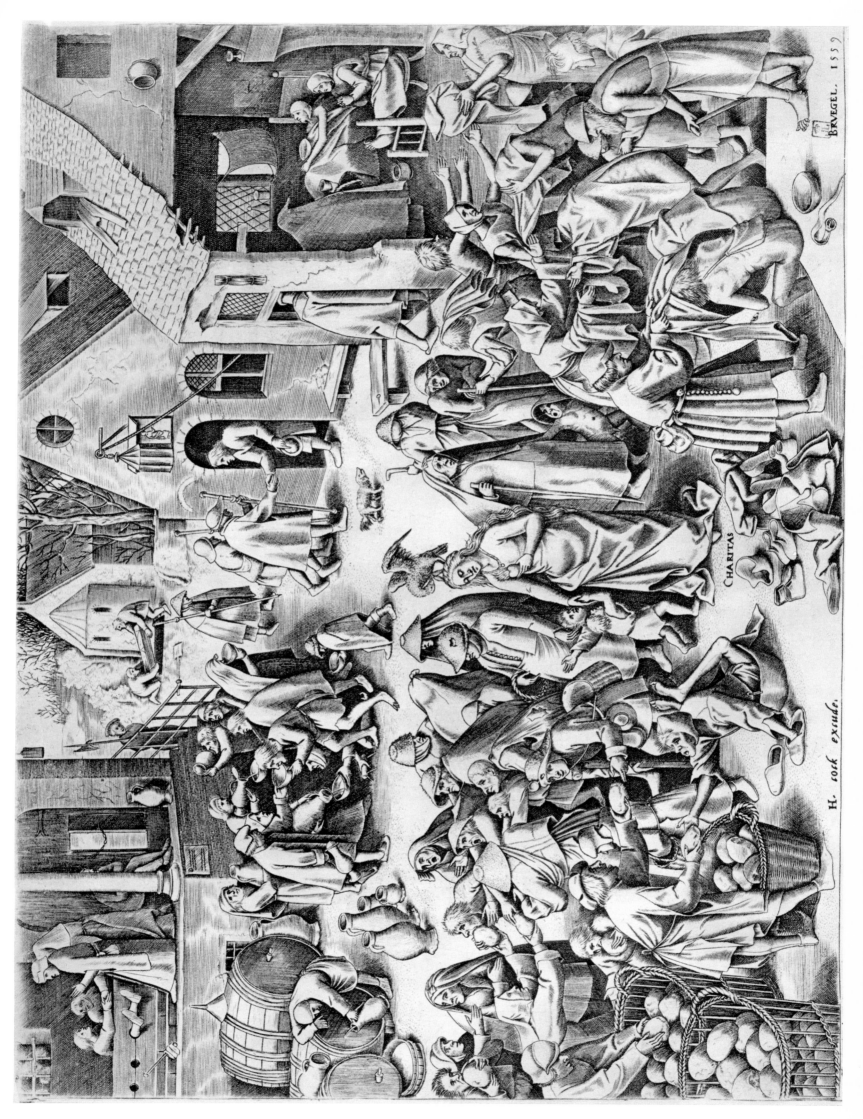

CHARITAS

BRVEGEL. 1559

H. cock excude.

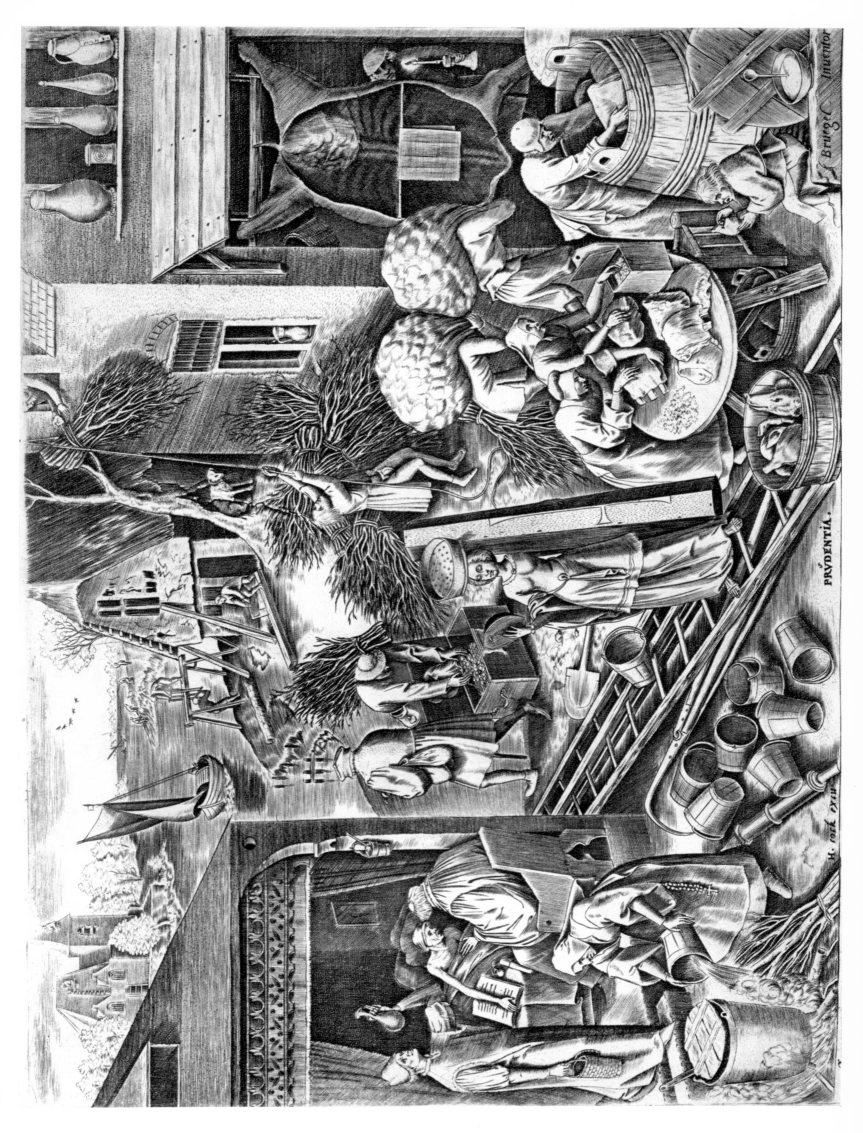

FORTITVDO·

COCK·EXC

BRVEGEL INVENTOR

67

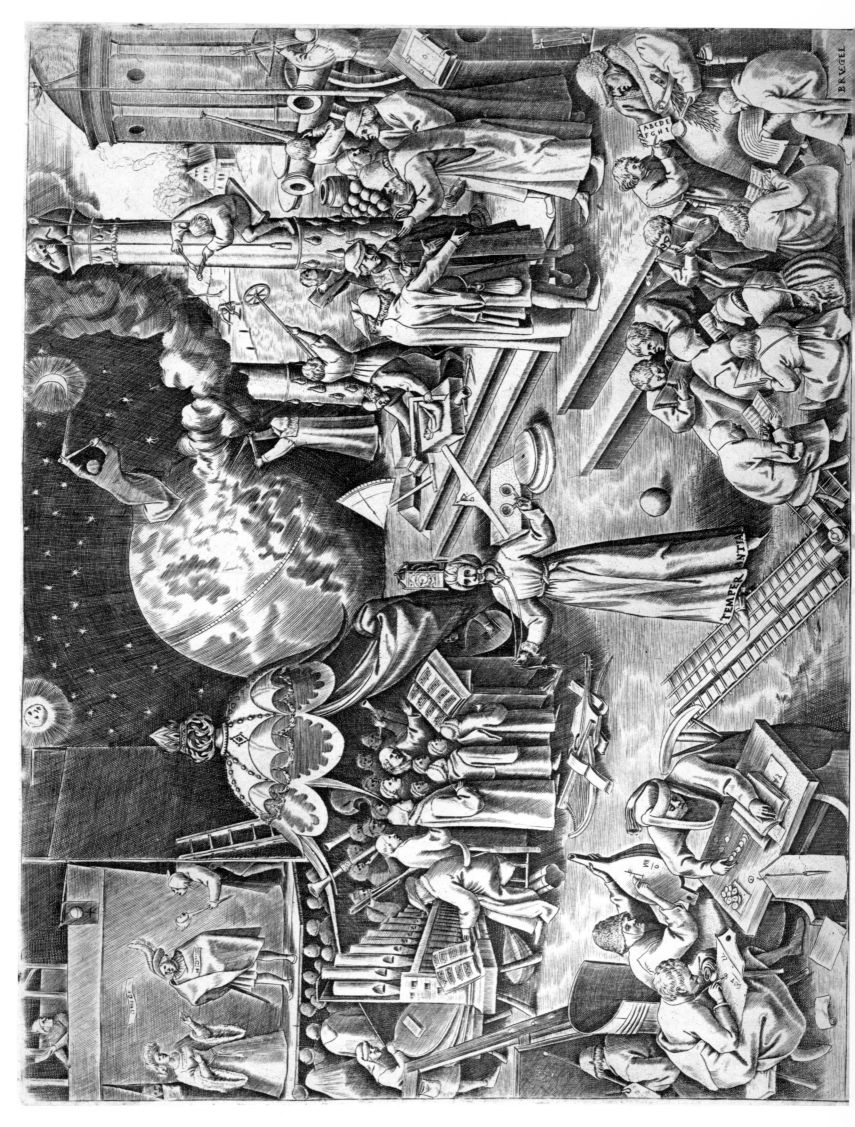

69

70

71

72

73

74

75

76

77

78

79

80

81

82

83

84

85

86

87

H COCK EXCV

88

H COCK EXCV

89

90

91

H cock excu

92

93

94

95

96

97

98

99

100

101

102

103

104

105

106

107

108

109

110

111

112

FRETI SICVLI SIVE MAMERTINI VVLGO EL FARO DI MESSINA OPTICA DELINEATIO

MESSINA

REZO

113

114

Bruegel, in, 1561.

115

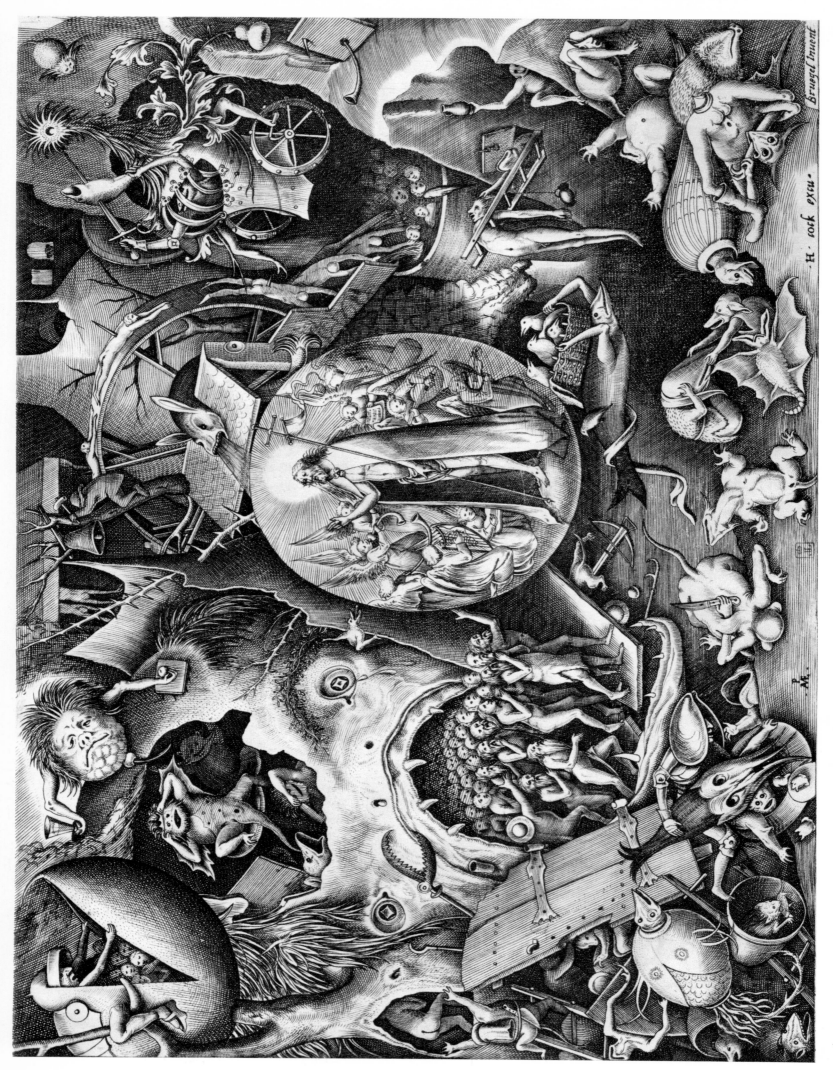

H. cock ex

brueghel inue 1563

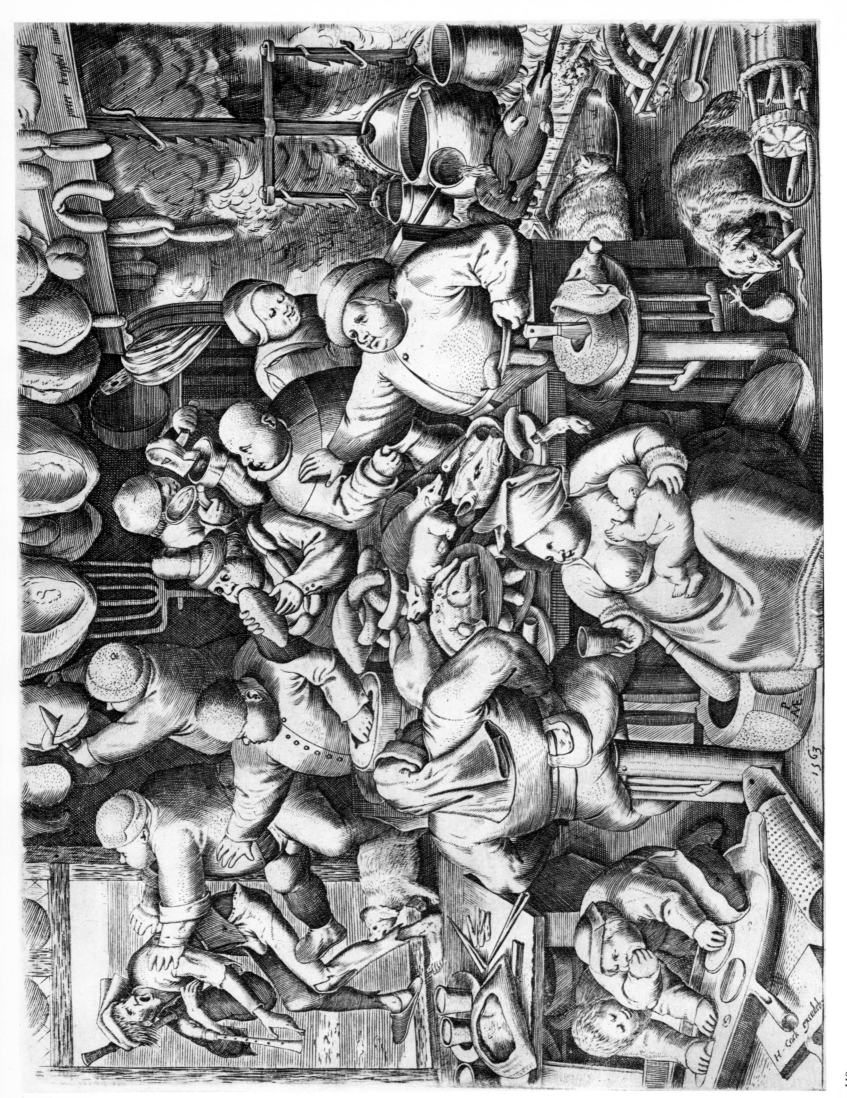

Aux quatre Vents.

P. Bruegel Inue

VERTOONINGE

Hoe de Pelgerimmen, op S. Ians-dagh, buyten Bruſſel, tot
Meulebeeck danſſen moeten; ende als ſy over deſe Brugh gedanſt hebben, ofte
gedwongen werden op deſe volgende maniere, dan ſchijnen ſy, voor
een Iaer, van de vallende Sieckte, geneſen te zijn.

Voor aen gaen deſe Speel-lieden ofte Moeſelaers, ſpeelende op Sack-pijpen; daer nae
volgen de Pelgrims, die met ſtercke Huyslieden gevat worden, ſeer ongaerne tegen haren wil [gelijck
in de tweede ende derde volghende Figuere vertoont wert] ſom krijtende en roepende; maer
komende ontrent de Brugge, ſoo keerenſe haer om, ende gebruycken groot tegenweer;
maer gevat zijnde, werden over de Brugge geheft ende gedragen; over zijnde
ſitten neder als vermoeyt weſende: ende dan komen de Huyslieden
van dier plaets, haer lavende, ende wat warms in-gevende:
ende is ſoo dit werck vol-eyndt.

Seer aerdigh uyt-gebeeldt door den uytnemenden konſtigen Schilder Pieter Breugel. *Geſneden ende gedruckt
ten Huyſe van* Henricus Hondius, *in 'sGraven-Hage,* 1642.

P. Breugel inv.   Hi. fec. Cum priv. 1642.

120

121   P.B. inv.   Hi fecit. 1642. Cumpriv.

122   Pet. Breug. inv. Hiondius fecit.   C. privil.

P:B: inv.   Hh: sculp. Cum priv.

123

1565

H. Cock exc.

Com priuilegio

FH

126

F·H· Bruegel

131

133

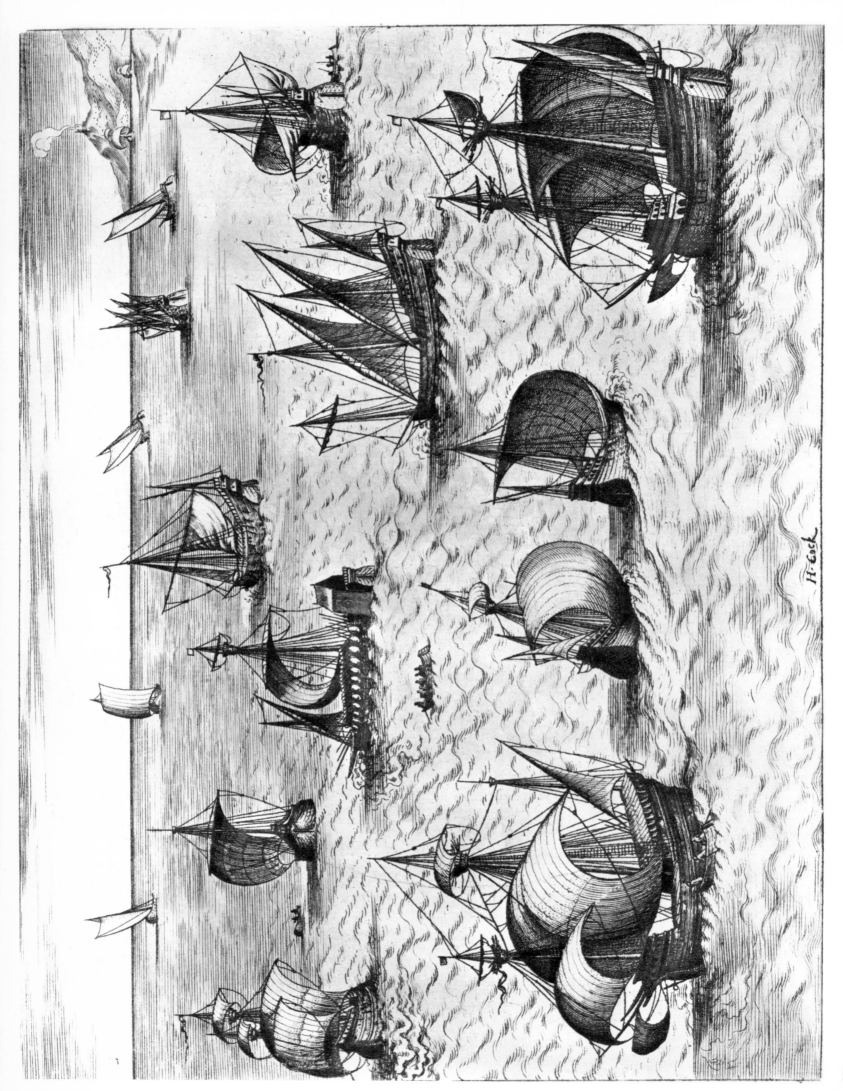

H·Cock

135

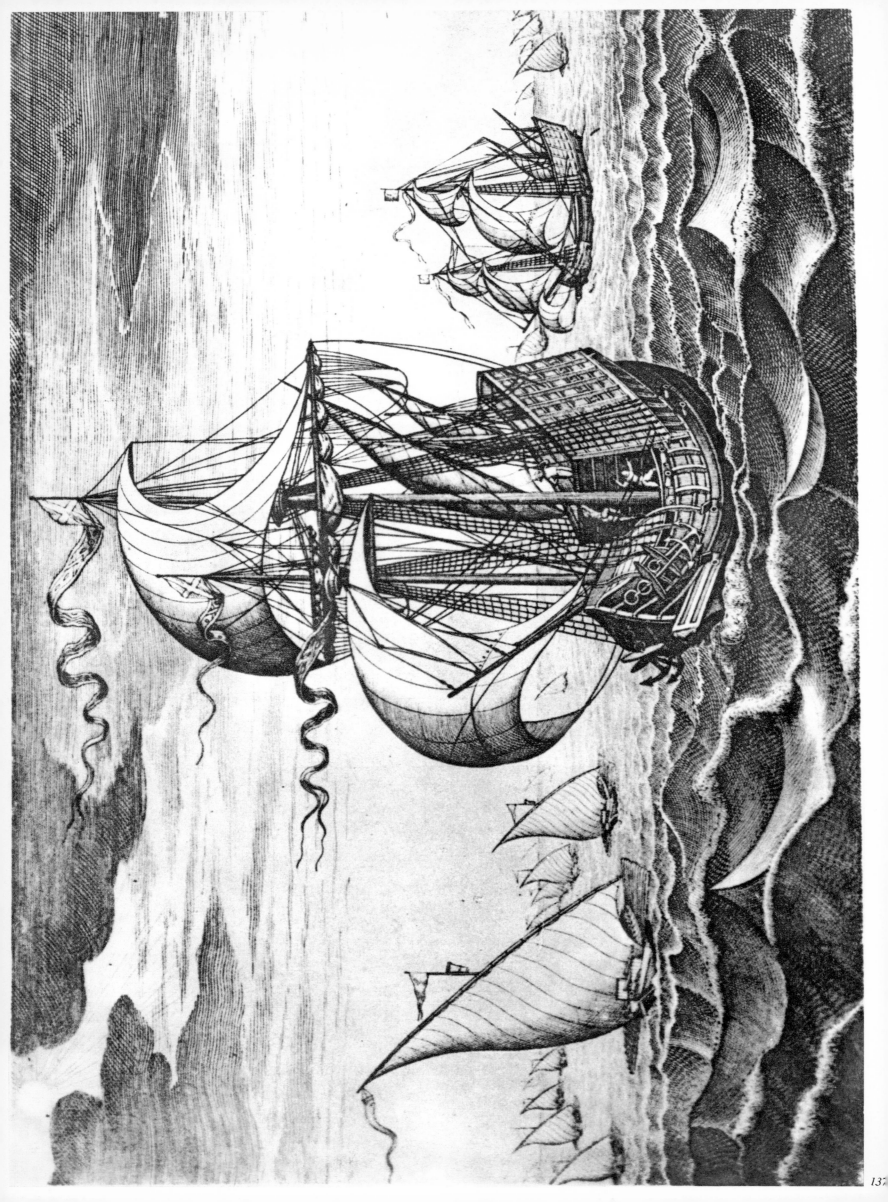

Bruegel · inuent.

cock · excudebat · 1555

138

Cock excudebat. 1565.

Bruegel. Inuent.

139

BRVEGEL · M · D · LXV.   P. Perret · fecit · 79 ·

DIE SONDER SONDE IS

Cum Priuilego.

140

144

BRVEGEL

145

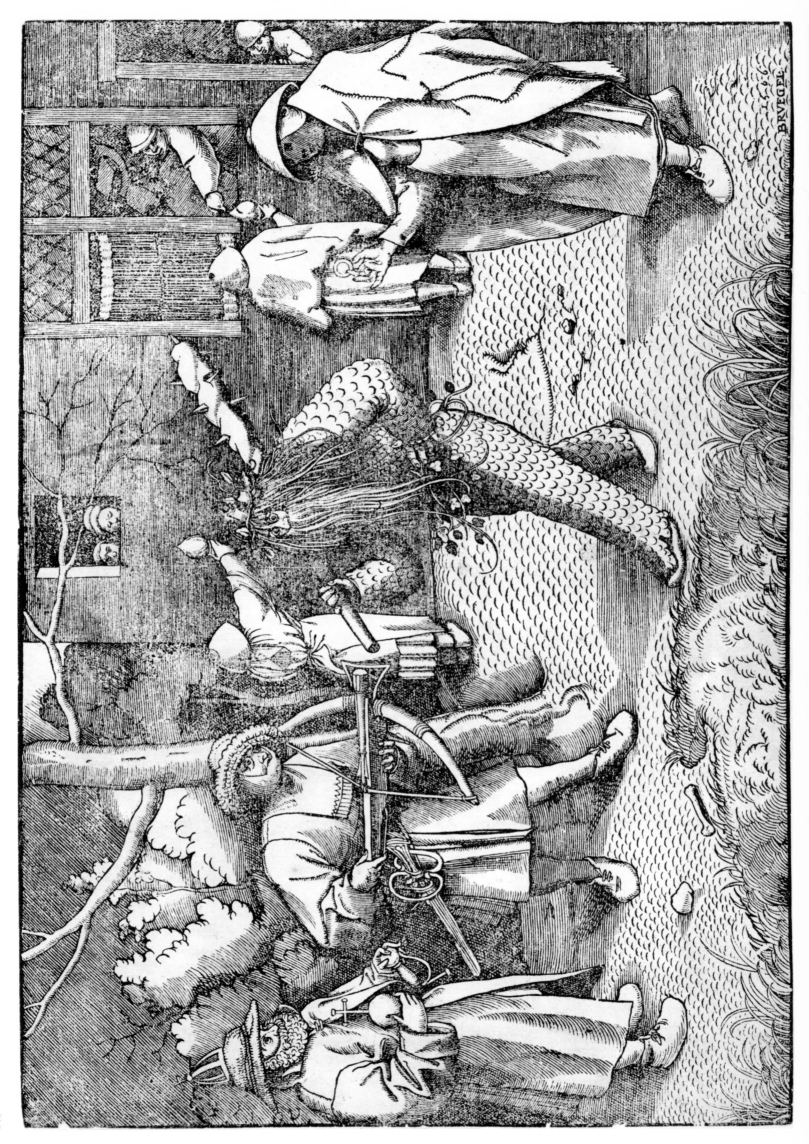

147

AESTAS Adolescentie imago. Frugiferas aruis fert Aestas torrida messeis.

Iulius, Augustus, nec non et Iunius Aestas.

INSVLA FORTVNATA.   LE PAIS GVLEVX ET PARESSEVX.
Abícondit piger manus fub afcellá fuá, et   Le parefeux cache fes mains foubz fon gofelet,
laborat ſi ad os ſuum eas converterit. Prov.26.19.   et luy eſt peine de les tourner vers ſa bouche.

HET LVY LECKER-LANDT.
Den luijaert breght ſijn handen onder ſijne ockſelen,
ende i⁰ valt hem ſuer, dat hyſe tot mondenwaerts heſſe.

149

150

Een leckende dack, ende een roockende schouwe, Is ongheluck in huijs, ja quellinghe en verdriet. Sa daer af Sinne vreit sit en tvay varuan sitt, en tvaiende sinne, een tvaiende sinne, Maer een tvaiende vrouwe.

Femme qui tanse sans raison,
Ne fait quenuÿ a la maison.
IH. VV.

151

Je porte dueil voyant le monde,
Qui en tant de fraudes abonde.

153

Tis goet Ontfangher sijn, inden Crijch principael, Hij caft een Afslaet en men laudeert sijn sake, Wi +/- is sijn dagie groot noch weet hij sijn waet, Hij hout hem heerlijck en speelt op die kake, +

Qui de recevoir a moyen,
Sur la madaire li iue bien.

A. Hier netten ende trompen ja oock schoon fluijten, Gheen beter waere men nu hier in d'landt en vindt. B. Weet versiä e Cremer coopt elaers struijten, Daer t'volck noch is hoorende doof en siende blindt. ✚

A. Voicÿ des vets trôpes et fleutes: Telle denrée onques vous neutes.
B. Va ten mercier va ten dicÿ: Ven ailleurs ta denrée aussi.

155

Wat ick clop, oft bid, tis voor een doofmans deure, Ons proue voort soer, ons cappe die versijt, Eijlaes, hebben wij tbeste nu ghetzen veure, Soo wil ick mij, den bedelsack haest maken quijt. ✠

Maintenant en vain nous mendions,
Car a lhuijs du sourd nous crions.

156

Qui souuent donne et rien a ioye,
Luneflesche vpres l'autre enuoye.

157

Sietmense beij tsamen inde gracht vallen. ✠ Wandelt altijt in alle voorsichtigheijt,

Sijt ghetrou/betrout niemant/dan Godt in allen:

Want om det aen . . . blinde dander leijt

158

Foey v verbuyckte dronckaerts sot, Altijt soer en suypt, vol tot den croppe: Op v vuijl en vrinckende als een marot, Ten lesten inden ijdelen doppe

Wie met bedroch sijn craem stoffeert, ⊹ Bij de bruijt sittende craut sijn noot
Leseu met pouer logeert, Voorwaer hij ten ... En also meijnt te ghewinnen rijckdom groot. Voorwaer hij ten ...

160

Daer thoij den peerde nae loopt is verkeert waert gheschiet, Merckt ghij dochters die selft aensoeckt soo ombeschaemt, De Jongmans te vrijen, tunwer eeren niet, Maer als tpeert thoij soeckende, uwer eeren betaemt. ✠

Als hy hem mach by de colen wermen. ✝ De sulck erghenbaerghiench met onuerstant, Soeckt elck bedecktens sonder onisermen, Hem en niets wers huys dat brant,

Bruegel · inventor ·

H. Cock excud · 1570 ·

P. Brvegel Inventor

1571

P. Gal. Fe.

BRVEGEL INVEN.
COCK. EXCV DEBAT.

166

167

168

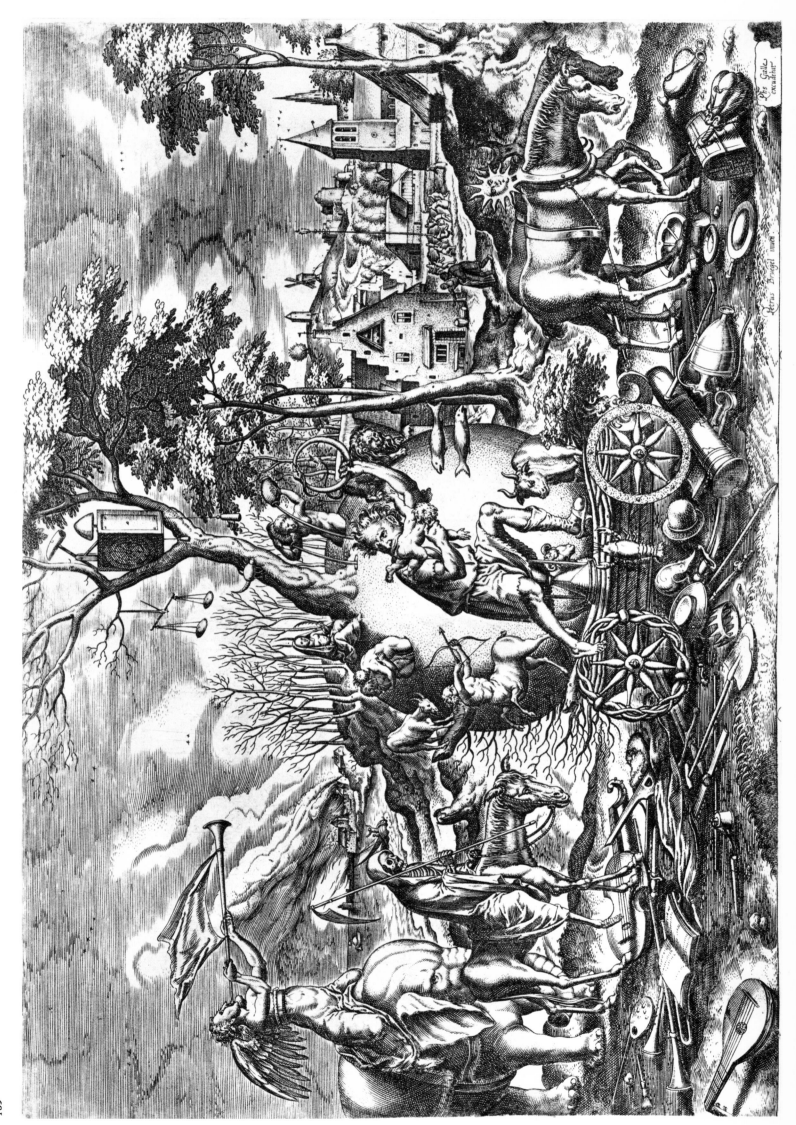

Pieter Breughel Pinxit   Cum Privil

170

172

173

LUCAS VAN LEYDEN

LIST OF WORKS REPRODUCED

All the engravings are reproduced in their actual dimensions, except those larger than the size of the volume itself. In this case, the reader will find a reduced reproduction and then a detail in the dimensions of the original, as well as the mention of the actual size of the plate. The dimensions are given height × width.

All the copper engravings and woodcuts of Van Leyden and those that can be attributed to him are reproduced. The mention of each work is followed by a capital letter referring to a catalogue of the engravings by Lucas van Leyden, the title of which is given in full in the Bibliographical Note: B: Bartsch; V: Volbehr; H: Hollstein; D: Dodgson.

The reproductions are taken from the first state except those specifically mentioned as being made from a second state.

When engravings bear no date, they are grouped by various criteria under dates generally accepted by scholars. A few independent woodcuts cannot be placed with sufficient accuracy in the chronology of Van Leyden and appear with the note "Undated."

The reproductions appearing in this work were made from the best proofs that we could photograph. We have made no corrections of possible faults that occurred in the printing of these proofs.

PIETER BRUEGEL THE ELDER

LIST OF WORKS REPRODUCED

All the engravings are reproduced in their actual dimensions, except those larger than the size of the volume itself. In this case, the reader will find a reduced reproduction and then a detail in the dimensions of the original, as well as the mention of the actual size of the plate. The dimensions are given height × width.

All the engravings by Pieter Bruegel and those that can be attributed to him are reproduced; these are all copper engravings with the exception of one woodcut. The listing of each work is followed by the initials V. B., which refer to the catalogue drawn up in 1908 by R. van Bastelaer.

The reproductions are taken from the first state, except those specifically mentioned as being taken from another version.

As the engravings were made from drawings that Bruegel often dated, it is those indications that have served as the basis of the chronology of the works.

The reproductions appearing in this work were made from the best proofs that we could photograph. We have made no corrections of possible faults that occurred in the printing of these proofs.

◄ *Please fold out*

LUCAS VAN LEYDEN

LUCAS VAN LEYDEN

LUCAS VAN LEYDEN

LUCAS VAN LEYDEN

LUCAS VAN LEYDEN

146	St. Anthony the Hermit	*B. 116*	*1521*	*Rijksmuseum, Amsterdam*
147	St. Christopher Carrying the Child Jesus	*B. 109*	*1521*	*Rijksmuseum, Amsterdam*
148	The Virgin and the Child Jesus in Glory	*B. 82*	*1523*	*Rijksmuseum, Amsterdam*
149	The Virgin with the Child Jesus, Seated at the Foot of a Tree with Two Adoring Angels	*B. 84*	*1523*	*Rijksmuseum, Amsterdam*
150	The Dentist	*B. 157*	*1523*	*Rijksmuseum, Amsterdam*
151	Old Woman with a Bunch of Grapes	*B. 151*	*1523*	*Rijksmuseum, Amsterdam*
152	The Murder of Abel	*B. 13*	*1524*	*Rijksmuseum, Amsterdam*
153	Lamech and Cain	*B. 14*	*1524*	*Rijksmuseum, Amsterdam*
154	The Surgeon and the Peasant	*B. 156*	*1524*	*Rijksmuseum, Amsterdam*
155	The Musicians	*B. 155*	*1524*	*Rijksmuseum, Amsterdam*
156	Virgil Suspended in a Basket	*B. 136*	*1525*	*Rijksmuseum, Amsterdam*
157	Self-Portrait of the Artist	*B. 173*	*1525*	*Rijksmuseum, Amsterdam*
158	St. Peter and St. Paul Conversing in a Landscape	*B. 106*	*1527*	*Rijksmuseum, Amsterdam*
159	Two Children Carrying a Helmet and a Flag	*B. 165*	*1527*	*Rijksmuseum, Amsterdam*
160	Two Genii Holding a Coat of Arms with a Mask	*B. 167*	*1527*	*Rijksmuseum, Amsterdam*
161	Ornament with the Head of a Soldier in a Circle	*B. 160*	*1527*	*Rijksmuseum, Amsterdam*
162	Ornament with Two Dolphins Facing Each Other	*B. 161*	*1527*	*Rijksmuseum, Amsterdam*
163	Venus and Cupid *(2nd state)*	*B. 138*	*1528*	*Rijksmuseum, Amsterdam*
164	Ornament with Two Sphinxes Back to Back on Either Side of Mercury	*B. 162*	*1528*	*Rijksmuseum, Amsterdam*
165	Ornament with Two Sirens	*B. 164*	*1528*	*Rijksmuseum, Amsterdam*

THE STORY OF THE FIRST COUPLE

166	The Creation of Eve	*B. 1*	*1529*	*Rijksmuseum, Amsterdam*
167	God Forbids the Eating of the Fruit of the Tree	*B. 2*	*1529*	*Rijksmuseum, Amsterdam*
168	Original Sin	*B. 3*	*1529*	*Rijksmuseum, Amsterdam*
169	The Expulsion of Adam and Eve from the Garden of Eden	*B. 4*	*1529*	*Rijksmuseum, Amsterdam*
170	The Murder of Abel	*B. 5*	*1529*	*Rijksmuseum, Amsterdam*
171	The Lamentation of Adam and Eve over the Body of Abel	*B. 6*	*1529*	*Rijksmuseum, Amsterdam*
172	Original Sin	*B. 9*	*1529*	*Rijksmuseum, Amsterdam*
173	Lot and His Daughters	*B. 16*	*1530*	*F. Lugt Collection, Institut Néerlandais, Paris*
174	Mars, Venus, and Cupid	*B. 137*	*1530*	*Rijksmuseum, Amsterdam*

THE THEOLOGICAL AND CARDINAL VIRTUES

175	Faith	*B. 127*	*1530*	*Rijksmuseum, Amsterdam*

LUCAS VAN LEYDEN

LUCAS VAN LEYDEN

LUCAS VAN LEYDEN

LUCAS VAN LEYDEN

277	St. Roch *(in Missale... T.)*	D. *47*	*1511–15*	*Bisschoppelijk Museum, Haarlem*
278	St. Sebastian *(in Missale... T.)*	D. *48*	*1511–15*	*Bisschoppelijk Museum, Haarlem*
279	St. Stephen *(in Missale... T.)*	D. *49*	*1511–15*	*Bisschoppelijk Museum, Haarlem*
280	St. Apolline *(in Missale... T.)*	D. *50*	*1511–15*	*Bisschoppelijk Museum, Haarlem*
281	St. Barbe *(in Missale... T.)*	D. *51*	*1511–15*	*Bisschoppelijk Museum, Haarlem*
282	St. Catherine of Alexandria *(in Missale... T.)*	D. *52*	*1511–15*	*Bisschoppelijk Museum, Haarlem*
283	St. Mary Magdalen *(in Missale... T.)*	D. *53*	*1511–15*	*Bisschoppelijk Museum, Haarlem*
284	St. Ursula *(in Missale... T.)*	D. *54*	*1511–15*	*Bisschoppelijk Museum, Haarlem*
285	St. Veronica *(in Ortulus anime...)*	D. *55*	*1511–15*	*Koninklijke Bibliotheek, The Hague*

SET OF FIVE RELIGIOUS ENGRAVINGS

286	The Nativity of Christ *(in Missale... T.)*	D. *3*	*1514*	*Bisschoppelijk Museum, Haarlem*
287	The Child Jesus *(in Missale... T.)*	D. *4*	*1514*	*Bisschoppelijk Museum, Haarlem*
288	The Resurrection *(in Missale... T.)*	D. *5*	*1514*	*Bisschoppelijk Museum, Haarlem*
289	Pentecost *(in Missale... T.)*	D. *6*	*1514*	*Bisschoppelijk Museum, Haarlem*
290	The Crowning of the Virgin *(in Missale... T.)*	D. *7*	*1514*	*Bisschoppelijk Museum, Haarlem*
291	Christ on the Cross, between the Virgin and St. John *(in Missale... T.)*	D. *1*	*1514*	*British Museum, London*

SET OF FIFTEEN RELIGIOUS ENGRAVINGS

292	Job and His Friends *(in Missale... T.)*	D. *13*	*1514–15*	*Bisschoppelijk Museum, Haarlem*
293	Christ on the Cross *(in Ortulus anime...)*	D. *14*	*1514–15*	*Koninklijke Bibliotheek, The Hague*
294	St. Matthew *(in Missale... T.)*	D. *15*	*1514–15*	*Bisschoppelijk Museum, Haarlem*
295	St. Mark *(in Missale... T.)*	D. *16*	*1514–15*	*Bisschoppelijk Museum, Haarlem*
296	St. Luke *(in Missale... T.)*	D. *17*	*1514–15*	*Bisschoppelijk Museum, Haarlem*
297	St. John the Evangelist *(in Missale... T.)*	D. *18*	*1514–15*	*Bisschoppelijk Museum, Haarlem*
298	St. Gregory *(in Missale... T.)*	D. *19*	*1514–15*	*Bisschoppelijk Museum, Haarlem*
299	St. Jerome *(in Missale... T.)*	D. *20*	*1514–15*	*Bisschoppelijk Museum, Haarlem*
300	St. Martin *(in Missale... T.)*	D. *21*	*1514–15*	*Bisschoppelijk Museum, Haarlem*
301	St. Nicholas *(in Missale... T.)*	D. *22*	*1514–15*	*Bisschoppelijk Museum, Haarlem*
302	St. Agnes *(in Missale... T.)*	D. *23*	*1514–15*	*Bisschoppelijk Museum, Haarlem*
303	St. Anne and the Virgin *(in Missale... T.)*	D. *24*	*1514–15*	*Bisschoppelijk Museum, Haarlem*
304	St. Dorothy *(in Missale... T.)*	D. *25*	*1514–15*	*Bisschoppelijk Museum, Haarlem*
305	St. Elizabeth of Hungary *(in Missale... T.)*	D. *26*	*1514–15*	*Bisschoppelijk Museum, Haarlem*
306	St. Margaret *(in Missale... T.)*	D. *27*	*1514–15*	*Bisschoppelijk Museum, Haarlem*

307	Duke Pepin of Brabant *(in Cronijcke...)*	D. *56*	*1517*	*Bisschoppelijk Museum, Haarlem*
308	St. Boniface *(in Cronijcke...)*	D. *57*	*1517*	*Bisschoppelijk Museum, Haarlem*
309	Thierry, First Count of Holland *(in Cronijcke...)*	D. *58*	*1517*	*Bisschoppelijk Museum, Haarlem*
310	The Miracle of St. Barbara at Gorkum in 1448 *(in Cronijcke...)*	D. *59*	*1517*	*Bisschoppelijk Museum, Haarlem*
311	The Emperor Charles V *(in Cronijcke...)*	D. *60*	*1517*	*Bisschoppelijk Museum, Haarlem*

SET OF SEVEN RELIGIOUS ENGRAVINGS

312	St. Dorothy	H. *38*	*1517 and 1528*	*British Museum, London*

LUCAS VAN LEYDEN

PIETER BRUEGEL THE ELDER

PIETER BRUEGEL THE ELDER

PIETER BRUEGEL THE ELDER

66	Prudence	V.B. 136	1559–60	Bibliothèque Albert I, Brussels
67	Fortitude	V.B. 137	1559–60	Bibliothèque Albert I, Brussels
68	Temperance	V.B. 138	1559–60	Bibliothèque Albert I, Brussels

SMALL LANDSCAPES OF BRABANT AND CAMPINE

69–112		V.B. 19–32, 34–63	1559–61	Bibliothèque Albert I, Brussels
113	Naval Battle in the Straits of Messina *(2nd state; 16½ × 27½″)*	V.B. 96	1561	Rijksmuseum, Amsterdam
114	Naval Battle in the Straits of Messina *(detail of fig. 113)*			
115	River Landscape with a Castle	V.B. 94	1561	Bibliothèque Albert I, Brussels
116	The Descent of Christ into Limbo	V.B. 115	1561	Bibliothèque Albert I, Brussels
117	The Poor Kitchen	V.B. 154	1563	Bibliothèque Albert I, Brussels
118	The Rich Kitchen	V.B. 159	1563	Bibliothèque Albert I, Brussels
119	The Battle of the Moneybags and the Strongboxes	V.B. 146	1563	Bibliothèque Albert I, Brussels

THE PILGRIMAGE OF THE EPILEPTICS TO THE CHURCH OF ST. JOHN AT MOLENBEEK

120	Two Bagpipe Players	V.B. 222	1564	Bibliothèque Albert I, Brussels
121	Two Fools	V.B. 225	1564	Bibliothèque Albert I, Brussels
122	Three Fools	V.B. 226	1564	Bibliothèque Albert I, Brussels
123	Groups of Pilgrims Walking toward the Right	V.B. 223	1564	Bibliothèque Albert I, Brussels
124	Groups of Pilgrims Walking toward the Left	V.B. 224	1564	Bibliothèque Albert I, Brussels

WARSHIPS

125	A Man of War	V.B. 98	1564–65	Bibliothèque Albert I, Brussels
126	A Man of War Armed with Cannons, Seen from behind at an Angle *(2nd state)*	V.B. 99	1564–65	Bibliothèque Albert I, Brussels
127	A Man of War, Seen from behind at an Angle	V.B. 100	1564–65	Bibliothèque Albert I, Brussels
128	A Man of War, Seen from behind at an Angle *(2nd state)*	V.B. 101	1564–65	Bibliothèque Albert I, Brussels
129	Man of War, Seen in Profile Sailing Toward the Left	V.B. 102	1564–65	Bibliothèque Albert I, Brussels
130	Man of War at Anchor, with Her Prow on the Right	V.B. 103	1564–65	Rijksmuseum, Amsterdam
131	Three Men of War, with Furled Sails	V.B. 104	1564–65	Bibliothèque Albert I, Brussels
132	Three Men of War in a Storm *(2nd state)*	V.B. 105	1564–65	Bibliothèque Albert I, Brussels
133	Man of War, Seen from the Poop, between Two Galleys, with the Fall of Phaëton	V.B. 106	1564–65	Bibliothèque Albert I, Brussels
134	Man of War, Seen from the Poop, between Two Armed Galleys	V.B. 107	1564–65	Bibliothèque Albert I, Brussels
135	Sixteen Vessels of All Kinds	V.B. 108	1564–65	Bibliothèque Albert I, Brussels
136	Four Men of War and Three Small Craft		1564–65	Stirling Collection, Keir (Scotland)
137	Flotilla of Small Vessels		1564–65	Stirling Collection, Keir (Scotland)
138	St. James and the Magician Hermogenes	V.B. 117	1564–65	Bibliothèque Albert I, Brussels
139	The Fall of the Magician Hermogenes	V.B. 118	1564–65	Bibliothèque Albert I, Brussels
140	Jesus and the Adulteress *(2nd state; 10½ × 13½″)*	V.B. 111	1564–65	Bibliothèque Albert I, Brussels

PIETER BRUEGEL THE ELDER